PRAISE FOR *PSYCHIC SKILLS FOR MAGIC & WITCHCRAFT*

"Crone wisdom resonates throughout the pages of this vital book that is certain to become a modern classic. Bringing together a lifetime of clinical and priestess training, Cat Gina Cole has written the consummate book for developing and growing psychic awareness and sensitivity."

—Katrina Rasbold, author of *Uncrossing* and *Crossroads of Conjure*

"I've read a *lot* of books on psychism, but this one is unique; not merely theoretical, but actual tried-and-true practical exercises, definitions, and explanations. Cat Gina Cole has organized solid lessons she has learned and now teaches into an easy-to-understand course of authentic study for both beginning and advanced practitioners. Her book presents foundational psychic skills for daily living in all forms of spiritual practices and I highly recommend it!"

—Oberon Zell, Headmaster of the Grey School of Wizardry and author of *Grimoire for the Apprentice Wizard*

"If you want to develop your intuition and related mental acuities, this is a fabulous resource! Each chapter provides a variety of tools, both material and otherwise, that allow you to open your mind and increase your focus. Even if you've never done any sort of psychic practice, this book will offer you the framework you need to get started and get better without being overly dogmatic or prescriptive."

—Lupa, creator of *The Tarot of Bones* deck and book

PSYCHIC SKILLS

for MAGIC & WITCHCRAFT

PSYCHIC SKILLS for MAGIC & WITCHCRAFT

Developing Your Spirit, Intuition & Clairvoyance

CAT GINA COLE

LLEWELLYN PUBLICATIONS
Woodbury, Minnesota

Coley M. Davis Jr

ABOUT THE AUTHOR

Cat was raised in a magical system by her mother and grandmother, and they initiated her into the family tradition at age thirteen. Over the years her grandmother taught her the ways of a Hedge Witch, Wortcunning, and "The Knowing," which is a mix of clairsentience, personal gnosis, and psychic ability.

From working in the garden with her grandmother, Cat became passionate about herbal medicine. Her insights about this are often discussed in her Facebook group Herbal Alchemy.

Cat's mother, being less traditional, and being a progressive -minded Christian Mystic. Cat's mom taught her interfaith morals and taught her to be an avid reader. Cat's literary education in the craft began at age ten with authors such as Edgar Cayce, Marion Zimmer Bradley, Lobsang Rampa, and many more.

By the age of eighteen, Cat was adept in clairvoyance, UPG, dreamwork, astral travel, mediumship, and empathic skills. She went on to use those skills in her work as a Dual Diagnosis counselor when inspired by Judith Orloff's book *Second Sight.*

During her fifteen years of counseling, Cat worked in such places as the Salvation Army ARC, the city detox, methadone clinics, and The Native Nations in Portland, Oregon.

Cat later stepped into the public arena of Paganism at age fifty through Rowan Tree Pagan Ministries. There, she began teaching and became an ordained Pagan Minister and High Priestess. Later Cat ran RTPM as a public organization for five years before going non-public.

She now hosts a private initiatory coven and school by the name The Coven of the Rising Phoenix where she teaches and is Co-High Priestess with Phaedra Bonewits.

In February 2020, Oberon Zell added Cat to the Grey Council, and Cat began writing for his magazine, *The Green Egg,* where she now has her own column that comes out quarterly. The magazine and her articles can be ordered at www.greeneggmagazine.com. Later that same month, Cat secured her book contract with Llewellyn.

Cat's hobby is helping the greater Pagan community. To this end, she created and admins The Rouge Valley Pagans Group, The Klamath Falls Pagan Spiritual Group, The Grants Pass Pagans Group, and The Elders and Leaders Group. Cat's main page on Facebook is Earth Witch Cat Gina Cole, where she is happy to chat with anyone who has questions. You can also follow her on Instagram and Twitter or follow her blog at catginacole.com.

First Edition
First Printing, 2022

Book design by Colleen McLaren
Cover design by Kevin R. Brown

Llewellyn Publications is a registered trademark of Llewellyn Worldwide Ltd.

Library of Congress Cataloging-in-Publication Data
Names: Cole, Cat Gina, author.
Title: Psychic skills for magic & witchcraft : developing your spirit, intuition & clairvoyance / Cat Gina Cole.
Other titles: Psychic skills for magic and witchcraft
Description: First edition. | Woodbury, Minnesota : Llewellyn Publications, 2022. | Includes bibliographical references and index.
Identifiers: LCCN 2021051620 (print) | LCCN 2021051621 (ebook) | ISBN 9780738767680 | ISBN 9780738767789 (ebook)
Subjects: LCSH: Psychic ability. | Parapsychology. | Magic. | Witchcraft.
Classification: LCC BF1031 .C588 2022 (print) | LCC BF1031 (ebook) | DDC
133.8—dc23/eng/20211104
LC record available at https://lccn.loc.gov/2021051620
LC ebook record available at https://lccn.loc.gov/2021051621

Llewellyn Publications
A Division of Llewellyn Worldwide Ltd.
2143 Wooddale Drive
Woodbury, MN 55125-2989
www.llewellyn.com

Printed in the United States of America

This book is dedicated to Jasper V.,
my grandson, who I love more than life itself,
and to Michael J. Keppers, my husband
and number one fan.

CONTENTS

EXERCISES

CHAPTER 1

CHAPTER 2

CHAPTER 3

CHAPTER 4

CHAPTER 5

CHAPTER 6

CHAPTER 7

CHAPTER 8

CHAPTER 9

ACKNOWLEDGMENTS

This book began with the life I led, and words cannot express the gratitude I have for my mother and grandmother. They taught me the family tradition of Psychism, Witchcraft, and Magic. Mom shared every book she ever read with me no matter how old I was. She taught me to love all people, to be open-minded, kind where possible, and brutal where needed. Their support and encouragement kept me going through a difficult life.

I would like to thank all the friends I had while growing up. Over the years, they tolerated my weirdness and came to recognize and respect my skills, which means the world to me.

Thank you to Aylah Hallel and all those in Rowan Tree Pagan Ministries. They educated me, helped me, gave me acceptance and friendship. Most of all, they helped me keep grounded after my mom died.

A special thank you to James Cooper, who connected my psychism to the cosmos and the great beyond in the most unique ways.

Thank you to Jess Loflin, Heidi Sapper, and Donna Barney for your love, support, loyalty, and belief in me; you have been my sounding boards and reality checks over many years.

To Katrina Rasbold, Phaedra Bonewits, Oberon Zell, and Rose Jacobs: I would never have gone to PantheaCon and pitched my book without you four encouraging me to do so. Thank you all so much for your part in that and for your continued support and friendship.

To Oberon Zell: I never thought I would get to know the Dumbledore of our time, and it is the greatest pleasure. Thank you for all your support, guidance, assistance, belief in me, your wisdom, and most of all your love. I look forward to many more years of sharing with you.

A very special mention and thanks to Phaedra Bonewits who has been my English lit teacher, proofreader, copyeditor, and career guide both in writing and Paganism. You have been my guidance counselor, friend sister, and partner. Mere words cannot describe my gratitude and love for all you are in my life.

Finally, to my husband, Michael Keppers, without whom this book would not exist. Thank you for insisting I keep every note I ever wrote, and for believing I was writing a book long before I ever did. You kept me going through it all and have been my number one fan in all I have accomplished. You have walked every step of it with me and I could not have done any of it without your dedication and fortitude. My respect, love, and gratitude for you are beyond measure; thank you for all you have done, and for sharing your life with me.

FOREWORD

BY PHAEDRA BONEWITS

Cat Gina Cole is my best friend. We met around 2014, a couple of years after I moved to Oregon. Poor health had kept me isolated, but once I met Cat, she introduced me to people, got me rides, and generally made sure I was included in local Pagan things. We wound up doing a lot of work together for a public Pagan group here in the Rogue Valley of Southwestern Oregon.

Our deep friendship may be surprising considering how different our talents and experiences are. She is from the rural Rogue Valley and learned a lot from mystics in her family. I am from Chicago and learned a lot through formal trainings and apprenticeships. We're an odd couple: city mouse and country mouse, homegrown Witchcraft and fancy learned stuff. But we mesh well enough to colead a coven.

Now here is where I embarrass myself. I knew Cat taught classes and took private students, but I had assumed she was teaching your basic Wicca 101, same as so many other people do. Same as I have done. But sometimes when she talked about this student or that, the direction she was going and even the language she used left me a little confused. *Hey, I know I should know what she's talking about, right?*

Alas, no.

It wasn't until I helped her format a manuscript that I really got a grasp on her curriculum.

I discovered that Cat takes on what a lot of people assume can't be taught: *psychism*, aka *psychic skills.* I haven't come across a lot of people who teach foundational psychic skills. Trance, yes, but things like the *clair* senses, not so much. Maybe it's because there's an idea that you are either psychic or not (nope, we've all got a little psychism inside of us), or maybe it's because those who are psychic don't really know how they'd go about teaching it to someone else.

Cat figured it out. She created a system of lessons and exercises that give people the tools to pay attention to, expand, and grow their personal psychic experiences.

So, if you think you're not psychic, think again. This book will help you find and grow what was there all along.

For those of you who know you have psychic ability, this book will help you fine-tune those skills. And for those of you who find living with your psychism overwhelming, you will be taught skills to help you manage your psychic experiences.

Cat has always kept copious journals and lesson plans, so for years her friends have told her, "You're writing a book." And she would insist not. Surprise! Now her techniques for taking people into the beyond are available to everyone.

It's true the over-culture says if we hear voices (*clairaudience*) or see what's not in front of us (*clairvoyance*) there's something wrong. Nope. Be proud of your psychism. Come join the psychic circle; we've left a spot just for you.

INTRODUCTION

I have been asked many times how long I have been a witch and psychic; my honest reply is "I have never not been one." I was four years old when I had my first psychic experience. I had my first out-of-body experience when I was four, and my first memorable clairvoyant event occurred when I was around seven.

My magical foundation was laid and assisted by Mom, Dad, and Grandma White. My dad, an immigrant from Italy, had dreams and saw ghosts. When I was older, my mother told me my real father was Native American and Hispanic. She took the secret of who he was to her grave.

Supposedly, Grandma White was not a blood relative. However, she was the only grandma we knew since our biological grandparents had passed before we were born. Grandma White told stories about her family traveling the trail of souls out of Romania during a war and how her family settled in Wales and Ireland. She proudly claimed she and her family as Gypsy. When I was older, my mom hinted that she was indeed my real grandmother, but she never confirmed that fact.

So the way I see it, I have always been a child of mystery and possibilities, and Mom fueled that. Mom was a Christian practitioner of Witchcraft and psychism. Today we call that being a Christian Mystic, and she hid that well from the rest of the family. Grandma was much more traditional and less open-minded than Mom.

When I was nine, Grandma shuffled some funny-looking cards and asked me to tell her what I thought they meant. Later, I learned they were tarot cards. The next day, Mom explained what the "Craft" and psychism were, the "Craft" being Witchcraft. She told me I had the gift of sight and swore me to secrecy. I was never to let anyone know about my gifts because they would not understand and may harm me for them. I could not even tell my siblings. No one, which meant only Mom and Grandma were to know about my gifts. They began my education in the Craft when I was young and initiated me into the family tradition when I was thirteen. Through puberty and on up into my late twenties my clairvoyant skills were off the hook. I could walk into a crowded room and hear not only the actual conversations that were happening, but also the ones in people's minds. Someone could be with friends, and I would feel their loneliness and depression and much more.

During this time, my skills flooded in with little control. I learned and generously used the skills of charm, glamour, and enchantment to bend people to my will. Coupled with clairvoyance and little fear of anything, I became an untamed Fairy.

This is the state I was in when I was introduced to bikers, and oddly that is when I learned to calm down. The bikers made me feel safe. They were easy for me to deal with because they were a closed group with clear rules. They quickly came to appreciate, value, and use my skills. Within the group, I saw and knew everything but stayed in the background. Yet I was always present whenever they had to deal with others. If I had any doubts about a person, it was a no go. Later, for fear of my safety, my mom suggested I find another way to fit into the world.

And in order to fit into this world, I was pushed hard through social conditioning to put all my psychism and Magic behind me. It remained that way for about ten years. Then in the mideighties, my skills began to sporadically trickle back. And so it went with my psychic skills until my grandmother passed.

Shortly after Grandma passed, I enrolled in college and quickly became a rising star as a Dual Diagnosis counselor, which is a counselor of people who have both mental health issues and an addiction. My skills now restored and enhanced, I began using them with my clients. This gave my skills of clairvoyance and empathy a place and purpose.

During my fifteen years as a counselor working with people in the city detox and methadone clinics, and among those of the Native Nations in Portland, Oregon, I began to see a pattern and kept records of my findings. My notes proved that 40 percent of the clientele I saw did not have mental issues, but had spiritual, religious, or psychic issues that had not been addressed or expressed. This meant they were likely born a psychic, witch, profit, seer, messenger, or magical practitioner of some kind and had no idea; they just felt lost, confused, out of control, or broken.

My clinical work became the creating and testing ground for many of the exercises in this book. It is what motivated me to leave the clinic and become a spiritual teacher and guide. I knew I could reach more people on the street level.

During this time, I learned three lessons: all things are temporary, what balance really is, and moderation in all things.

In 2018, I lost my psychic skills because of a car accident in which I received a head injury. This traumatic time in my life made me wish for an instruction manual I could use to regain my psychic skills. Then I remembered all the lessons I had previously written and taught, and I realized this was the manual I needed to regain my skills. So while I cannot write an instruction manual for regaining psychic skills specific to everyone, I can write one to help others based on my own experiences.

Because of my experiences I know how important it is to find something and someone you can relate to and identify with as a psychic. This is something I intentionally wrote into these pages; I know being a psychic has many challenges, valid fears, and concerns to be dealt with, and I want you to know that you are not odd, a freak, or mentally ill for having psychic skills and being different.

THE STRUCTURE OF THIS BOOK

This book is based on a three-level curriculum I teach that progresses from beginner to intermediate and on to advanced skills. In each chapter are correctly labeled psychic skills, discussions, and examples of personal stories about how each skill works. Also, you will see what these practices look or feel like accompanied by tools and exercises that are easy to understand. The work in this book is a reference and a study course that will increase the effectiveness, skill, and confidence of any psychic.

Chapter 1 includes a brief chapter glossary with definitions to get you familiar with the terms used as you start your studies and there is a bibliography and index in the back of the book for further reference material.

To successfully complete the work in this book, you will need a journal. Writing down your thoughts and experiences is vital to your practice. You will see examples of my personal journal entries throughout that demonstrate a journal's value.

As a Hedge Witch, I focus on how psychic skills fit into Magic, Witchcraft, and ritual, but these skills by no means are exclusive to those areas. Anyone, not just magical practitioners or people of a specific religion or culture, can use the skills I present.

As you progress through the chapters and read about my experiences and knowledge, you will learn that being a psychic is a life journey and a life skill that is seldom taught. By writing this book, it is my desire to ease your journey. May this book be your guide and many blessings to all!

Chapter 1
PSYCHIC SKILL BUILDING

To be a psychic can be mysterious, alluring, and challenging. We each have a unique way in which our skills present and a unique way of interpreting or reading the information we receive. That said, there are three basic consistencies to all things psychic: thoughts, belief, and perspective. We begin with the most basic psychic tool, thoughts.

THOUGHTS ARE THINGS

Psychism is a dance between science and mystery, which cannot be separated because they are two parts of a whole. Knowing this assists in defining psychism clearly. Combining scientific explanation and mystery also gives us additional skills needed to practice psychism, because understanding the science and later adding your emotions will further enhance the effectiveness of the techniques.

Psychism is not tangible, and the first nontangible concept you must have is the *belief* that thoughts and emotions are real things with real energy, much like electricity. You can see the wires, but you cannot physically see the electricity.

For psychic skills, you need to believe it is possible to pick up the vibration, color, sound, energy, and visual resonance of thoughts and emotions because those are the vehicles for all things psychic.

All things psychic travel on, and are created by, or consist of, vibration and energy that emanate from thought, emotion, and perception. Science has proven that thoughts cause a vibration in our world. These vibrations create energy and leave behind a resonance in our bodies, minds, and senses as they move through us. Those vibrations are everywhere all the time—traveling like radio waves or light waves. And like those waves, thought and emotional waves can and do travel through our bodies. Some of those waves resonate within us stronger than others and stimulate unseen mental images and other perceptions and senses.

Have you ever walked into a hospital and noticed that the atmosphere just feels a bit different? Or walked into a room after an argument and felt it? Or walked into a church or temple and suddenly felt the sacredness of it? Those sensations are the tangible results of the nontangible vibrations and energies left over from thoughts and emotions as they resonate in the environment. We feel that resonance, but do we truly believe they are leftover energies of thoughts, emotions, and events?

BELIEFS

What you believe about energy and psychism is the second most important nontangible concept you need to examine to begin working in psychism. Belief is the power and conviction that fuels your thoughts. Belief creates the energy to your thoughts that then vibrate within you until they become actions and words.

For example, if you say you believe everyone has some psychic ability but then say to yourself, "Oh, that was just a coincidence" when something happens, what does that really say about your beliefs? When you have a psychic occurrence but dismiss it because it is socially awkward or unacceptable, this is a notice to you about your beliefs and is one that needs attention.

Fear and Beliefs

When you are afraid to express your beliefs, you can weaken the power behind that belief. This kind of fear can also weaken or block your psychic skills and their effectiveness. Many valid fears go with being psychic. There is the fear of losing control, which partners with the fear of the unknown; some people even fear the social impact.

I recommend looking at your fears about psychic skills with an open mind and addressing them through journaling at the beginning of your psychic journey. This will help you discover what fears and old beliefs you might need to let go of to open the door to your journey.

PERSPECTIVE AS A SKILL

Perspective is the third most important concept for a psychic to master. Perspective is the way you view or think about something. A new perspective can change your beliefs and how you feel about them. If you can change the way you view something, your beliefs will follow. And as your emotions change with those beliefs, many fears will subside.

These three concepts will assist you as you begin to practice and study. At this point, I recommend journaling on these concepts so you can clear the way as you study.

CHAPTER GLOSSARY OF TERMS

While some cringe at the word *study,* the best way I have found to study a text is to read the glossary before reading the book.

By reading the glossary first, I understand what is being said as I read. Following is a brief first-chapter glossary that defines the basic skills you will use as you study and practice. They may seem huge in concept to you now, but you will find they are relatively simple as you proceed.

Awareness

Observing or noticing the subtle details. This can be done with or without physical vision.

Balance

Balance is an easy word to understand in general. However, in psychism, it takes on a whole new meaning. In psychism, *balance* means to maintain a semblance of equity between your psychic and magical world experiences and your real-world experiences. The balance I speak of is the balance we must maintain as we experience walking in both worlds.

Daily living

Using your practiced skills daily because they are a part of how you live.

Faith

Faith is a knowing. A conviction or trust. An unshakable knowing of a concept or idea. Your perceptions and thoughts about concepts and ideas.

Imagination

A tool used in the creation of conceptual thinking using visualization, psychism, Magic, and Witchcraft. Imagination is letting the mind think what it wants with no restrictions.

Intuition

Sometimes defined as a gut instinct. For magical practitioners, it is the ability to hear or feel the higher mind, higher self, or inner spirit, or that small quiet voice inside and its guidance.

Journaling

Keeping notes on one's experiences, thoughts, feelings, study, and practices.

It never fails that when I ask students to keep a journal, they ask if they can keep a digital journal. The answer is no! Here is why. Handwriting is connected directly to your thought process. This thought process then flows through your body creating an embedded memory for both the mind and body. Handwriting stimulates the part of the creative brain in the cerebral cortex that a computer or other electronic device does not.

The part of the cortex that handwriting accesses is the very part of the mind we are trying to enhance in psychic skill building, and writing by hand puts the mind in a semi-altered state similar to spellwork and meditation. Typing on a device does not access the same part of your brain. Journaling also assists in making our thoughts more tangible and present in our lives and mind.

Journaling is how this book came into being and how my thoughts and experiences became tangible. I have been handwriting lessons and journaling for ten years. I have thirteen notebooks broken down into subjects and labeled. You may be thinking this system is a pain because it all had to go on the computer later. This, too, has its use.

When you enter your handwritten notes on the computer, you also are reading them, which then taps the deeper memories and thoughts that were previously provided in the original writing. This stimulates a more informative and consistent flow of thought, memory, and emotion. As you read your notes several times, you also will increase your memory retention.

As you journal, remember that only you need to be able to read the words. Your writing does not have to be excellent with proper punctuation and spelling. In fact, I advise against that. I encourage freewriting as you journal: just let it flow as it will. And of special note, journaling is also how a Book of Shadows begins.

Knowing yourself

Knowing yourself means you know what you are feeling, you know what your personality traits are like, and you have the ability to acknowledge them when they appear. To know yourself means you know yourself as a person so well you can tell what feelings and emotions belong to you and what does not in any given moment. This is a vital skill in psychism.

Meditation

A state of mind in which an individual achieves a theta state. In meditation, you clear and focus the mind to achieve calm, clarity, and information. Meditation is a method used to receive and experience visions and spiritual insights, and it requires the shifting of the consciousness into an altered state.

Pause

To calm all functions and thoughts. This is done by clearing the mind and putting the emotions on hold.

Pivoting

To turn your current thoughts to something else. Usually something more constructive or positive to distract yourself.

Practice

The effort you put into learning and becoming skilled. It is a discipline or devotion you put the time into, to master.

Psychic

Someone who can divine knowledge and information that is unseen by using other than normal means. A person who is sensitive to stimuli beyond the natural range of perception and current natural or scientific knowledge. A psychic's total mind and body can tune in to the subtle vibrational frequencies and decipher them for a practical purpose. A psychic can establish a neutral mind and hold an intense focus to enter an altered state of consciousness at will or as the need arises.

Psychic skills

The basic skills needed to achieve and develop a broad spectrum of psychic abilities. They are pause, sensing, scanning, imagination, meditation, and intuition.

Psychism

The study and practice of all things psychic. It includes all psychic skills and phenomena. Psychism is a lifelong practice and study. It is also an umbrella word used to include multiple psychic skills while in a conversation.

Scanning

To pause and investigate your mind and body to identify what you are feeling and why. You can also pause and cast your senses outward to sense and feel what is going on around you and with others.

Spiritual evolution

The process a person goes through on their spiritual journey, one that begins with looking at your beliefs and social conditioning and ends with gratefulness and gratitude.

Trust

Means you believe the information you receive, without question. Trust is believing in your ability and knowledge without any doubt. It also has been called having faith.

Visualization

The ability to focus with the aid of the imagination until the desired object can be clearly seen in the inner mind, effectively creating an image in the inner mind.

Now that you have a description of the basic psychic skills, let's explore them in more detail.

THE PAUSE SKILL

You may think pausing is no big deal, but in psychism it is essential. When psychics pause, it is to stop our thinking and our emotions, and to shut out the daily world around us. In this manner, we clear our minds so we can think. While in pause, you receive information from your consciousness and more. The pause skill is a tool used to stimulate your intuition and calm the emotions when needed and helps you gain access to the more advanced skills.

Pause Exercise

Find a quiet place where you know you will not be responsible for anything in the next few minutes. It can be the bathroom at work or home, a supply closet, just out the back door, or anywhere. Close your eyes and just breathe until you feel yourself relaxing. Release the day and world from your thoughts; keep breathing gently, and do this for at least five minutes.

When you get to a place of calm within you will know it. When you reach that place, breathe gently a couple more times, gather your thoughts, and you are done. Carry the relaxation and calm with you when you leave.

I recommend practicing pause as many times a day as you can and to journal or note in some fashion what you experience while you pause.

The goal of becoming skilled with the pause is to be able to use it when you are in the middle of something. The pause is helpful when you have lost your train of thought and when you are overwhelmed or stressed. Once skilled, you can pause just by closing your eyes and breathing without needing the quiet space to help you focus.

I use pause all the time in my teaching and while doing public rituals. As I began my path, I was so anxious speaking in public that I would stutter. Now, when I have something public to do, I close my eyes and use the pause exercise. This allows me to listen to my inner confident self and hear my thoughts. I often find with my students that having your eyes open can enhance anxiety, and that anxiety calms when the eyes are closed.

For example, at the Sacramento Pagan Pride in 2019, I was asked to call the quarters at the closing ritual. At first, I was nervous and afraid of messing it up. The first few words came easily, then I started to stutter. Right in mid-sentence I closed my eyes and paused. This calmed the anxiety. When I paused, the crowd repeated what I had previously said, which prompted me to move along and got the crowd involved in the ritual. So it worked beautifully, and it looked like it was planned that way.

Pause is a simple skill that can be extremely useful. When teaching, I use the pause to tap into my intuition or to think of what is right for the person I am speaking to. The pause also can be used in spells and Magic to let the energy build or settle down. It is also useful while using your intuition and psychism during scanning, meditation, visions, and trance.

You can practice pause at home using the following meditation. I recommend practicing each step of the meditation separately to master the skill. For all the meditation exercises, record them and play them back to yourself or have a friend read them and guide you through them. Be sure to do so with an easy pace and gentle tone.

Pause Meditation Practice

Sit quietly and comfortably in a chair with your feet on the floor. Close your eyes and let all tension flow from your body, gently breathing while you relax. With your inner mind, visualize or think about a star out in dark space. Now imagine, visualize, and feel a light beam from the star to the top of your head. Take your time to get a good visual or feel. Keep relaxing and breathing to allow yourself to begin to feel the tingling of the light as it connects to the top of your head. Now let the light surround your head, relaxing the scalp, ears, and jaw. As the light moves over you, it begins to feel like gently flowing warm water infused with starlight.

Let the watery light flow over you like a waterfall on a sunny day. Visualize the water flowing down and around your neck, taking all the tension with it as it flows. Breathe out the tension with the water as it flows over you. Now visualize the water flowing over your shoulders and down your back. Feel it take all the tension in your body with it. The water flows over your chest, down your arms, and down your fingertips, relaxing you.

Breathe gently as the lighted water flows over your belly, and down your back, removing all tension as it flows. Now let the lighted water fill up the space between your hips like a bowl and breathe with it there. Revel in how good it feels as the water now spills out over your pelvis and onto your thighs and bottom, relaxing them. Breathe gently as the water begins flowing down your legs and let them relax.

The water is now in your knees flowing through the joints of your knee. Relax the back of your knees and let the water wash down the calves of your legs, releasing the tension. You feel the water flowing around your calves, and around and through the joints of your ankles; let go and relax. As you gently breathe, the water now puddles around your feet. Visualize the water flowing over every bone in your feet and let them relax. Breathe gently and notice how relaxed your whole body is and enjoy it for a moment.

Your body now feels like it is asleep, but your mind is calm and aware. Now with your inner mind, gaze into the puddle at your feet. Let yourself get lost in it like a daydream. As you look at the puddle, notice its movement, shadows, and light. Breathe. This is the place of pause. Linger here for as long as you like.

When you are ready, visualize the lighted water rising back up your body from the puddle and swirling around you. As the water rises, it now wakes your body and tingles as it moves up each part of you. The water is flowing up your calves and over your knees, refreshing them, waking them. The water is now moving over your knees up your legs. As it fills your hips, breathe it in deeply and stay relaxed. The water now moves up your stomach; it wraps around your torso as it moves upward.

Feel each part of your body waking, tingling, and feeling refreshed. Breathe in the feel of the water as it wraps around your torso, waking your body. You now begin to feel the chair under you and your feet on the floor. Wiggle your toes and take a deep breath as you begin to wake. Now you feel the chair on your back and arms, and your hands are tingling; wiggle your fingers as they wake up.

The water is now around your chest and upper back, and you are fully aware of the chair you are in. Breathe in as you let the water flow over your head, waking the jaw and ears. When it reaches the crown of your head, it once again becomes a beam of light shooting back to the star. Feel that connection, and let it tingle there for a moment.

Now breathe and feel the chair and floor completely. Notice how relaxed you are. Wiggle your fingers and toes again. Take your time coming around. When you are ready, open your eyes and stretch in your chair.

Do not stand up right away. Some folks report feeling dazed and extremely relaxed after this exercise and can get dizzy if they stand up too fast. This is the time for self-care. Get something to drink and have a snack. This serves to bring your body back to full awareness and get it reorientated. I recommend this exercise at least once a week, more if you can.

THE SENSING EXERCISE

To sense, complete the pause exercise again. While in pause, let yourself now observe and feel the vibrations and energy around you. Check in with your body first. What is it feeling? If you are tense, ask your body why. It will tell you if you listen and relax.

Just notice and observe for now. Then move that information aside in your mind. Keeping your eyes closed, think of the room or space around you. How does that space feel? Stay with it for as long as you can and let yourself sense the energy and vibrations. What does it feel like? Is it humming? Does it feel still or heavy? Can you feel the presence of others? Do you hear anything? Do you see anything? When you are done, write about your experience.

It may take a while to write it all down. If you just feel calm and peace that is good, that is still sensing something. If you do not get anything the first time, do not worry. That is why it is called practice. If you are too stressed, hungry, or rushed for time, or if you are being too passive about stretching your senses, it can all affect you. So be gentle with yourself, be patient, and keep practicing.

Having a regularly scheduled time to practice helps to trigger your mind as you practice. I know we are all busy, but you must make time for practice, even if it is five minutes at a time because any practice time is good time.

To get good at sensing, do the pause exercise in many different places. A park, a grocery store, at work, at home, anywhere will do. Sense until you can feel the energy and vibrations, the weather, the sky around you, the air on your skin, the birds in the air, the feel of the plants, or the feel of the ground under your feet.

Practice pause and sense until you feel comfortable and you no longer need the relaxation meditation to accomplish it. These two steps are a good way to check in with the space around you anytime and set the groundwork for your intuition.

THE SCANNING SKILL

The difference between sensing and scanning is an important distinction. In scanning, you expand your sensing to discover the cause of what you are sensing. In sensing, you are just feeling what is around you without looking further.

To scan, you begin by using the pause, then the sense skill. By doing this, you shift your consciousness and awareness beyond your everyday mind into a premeditative state. Then you expand your awareness to scan for the energy or vibration, or activity that is causing you to sense something. The goal is to zero in on the cause of what is stimulating your senses. Note how stimulation from others feels different than when you sense just yourself or the environment.

Another method to practice scanning is to focus on just one object—a tree, a dog, most anything—until you feel its energy. Feel how its life force is different than yours.

The goal is to get to know the difference in feelings or stimuli that come from outside of you, compared to when it is just you. This skill is vital in getting to know the subtle differences in various psychic stimuli and increases accuracy.

Feeling other people's emotions and thoughts can be a bit overwhelming at first. It can be difficult to tell who is who. To deal with this, I began asking myself questions. Do I typically feel this way? Why would I be worried about this? Is it reasonable that I would feel this way? It is easier when I stick to the facts, such as whether this thing I feel is real in my life.

For example, when COVID-19 first hit our area, I was driving by a Walmart and was suddenly overcome with fear and anxiety about what I desperately needed to stock up on. It consumed me for a few minutes until I applied my reason and looked at the facts, which were that I had everything I needed. I had to recognize that these feelings were not mine but belonged to the people in the Walmart I was driving by. I had to do breathing exercises and talk myself down from the panic, yes, while driving.

This is an excellent example of why it is so important to know what is you and what is not. This type of self-care and awareness is key for sensitive people and psychics of all kinds.

Scanning can be done in a coffee shop or anywhere when you need it. You can intentionally scan a place before you enter, or a person you are sitting with. Keep notes on what this activity is like for you. What do you think you can do better? Keeping notes of what you experience will broaden your skills and self-knowledge and improve accuracy.

What other senses do you notice while scanning? This is an important question because scanning can open the door to your area of psychism. Maybe your inner hearing is better than your inner vision. Maybe you feel more like an empath does. Maybe you see colors or auras. Perhaps after you scan you later dream of what you have scanned. All those things are your subconscious talking to your conscious mind. If you dream of them, it is a type of dream clairvoyance.

There are many possible psychic skills and journaling will help you figure much of it out. So do keep track. You can look back on what you've written later and pick what stands out, or even what you would like to practice more.

Visualization Exercise 1, Part 1

The following visualization exercise will build your scanning skills.

Walk around in a familiar room that is completely dark as often as you can to train your mind and eyes. You can even do this while wearing a sleep mask or a blindfold.

As a child, I used to be fascinated with how cats could see in the dark, and I would walk around when the house was completely dark to discover how well I could see in the dark. While doing this eventually trained my eyes to see better in the dark, it also increased my ability to keep a visual image in mind much longer, and it is a habit I have kept. I found it primed my physical sight to see odd shapes in the shadows, which trained my brain to discern what those shapes were while staying calm long enough to do so. This skill now carries over into my psychism when I have visions or dream.

Visualization Exercise 1, Part 2

To take the first part of the exercise to an advanced level, look around the space you are in and notice every detail, how far things are from you, their placement, and so on. Then close your eyes or put on a sleep mask or blindfold.

Hold the image of what you saw firmly in your mind. Reach out and see if you can touch or walk around certain objects. Is the object where you saw it in your mind? Can you tell what it is by touching it? When you touch it, can you see it clearly with your inner vision? A slight peek now and then is okay as you practice. This exercise trains your mind in spatial relationships to objects, a skill you can then use in dreams or trance.

Visualization Exercise 2, Part 1

For this exercise, we will become one with an object. It will require deep visualization, relaxation, focus, sensing, and scanning. You will have to sense, visualize, and feel all at the same time, with gentle focus while staying calm.

Find a tree or other plant you can spend some quiet time with. To begin, release your daily stress, using the pause meditation, then move into the sense and scan, breathing gently. Let your mind go beyond your everyday mind as you consciously shift your consciousness.

Close your eyes and expand your awareness and senses outward toward the tree. Scan and sense until you feel the tree and its energy. Let the tree's energy into you and let it meld with you. Open your imagination and expand your senses. Feel its bark and smell its earthiness with your whole body, and feel what the tree is giving back. Take your time to really feel and experience each of these steps.

Now work your way up the trunk and breathe with the tree. Stay with it for a moment. As you notice the sensations, let them flow through you. Continue working your way up the tree and out to the tip of the branches. By the time you get to the tips, you should be feeling the tree so much, you will feel like raising your head and arms to catch the glorious sun in celebration. Enjoy it for a moment.

Begin bringing yourself back by concentrating on the feel of dirt under your feet.

Separate yourself from the tree by feeling all of your body. Breathe gently. When you are fully separated and can visualize yourself standing in front of the tree, gently take your time to come back to reality.

Visualization Exercise 2, Part 2

While standing before the tree or plant, begin with the pause and scan exercise. Take a breath and calm yourself. Gather your focus. Now push your focus and senses through the bark and into the wood; visualize it as you go until your consciousness is in the center of the tree. Sense for the spirit or soul of the tree; think of it as a being, and feel its personality. Now let yourself merge. Let your imagination take over the vision. Talk with the being of the tree or plant. Breathe. Let the experience happen for as long as you can. Be patient though—trees and plants speak slowly. Once you are finished, separate yourself and come back.

When I do this now, I get visions from the tree about how the area around it has changed over time. The trees often show me their memories and share insights and wisdoms.

You can practice this method with almost any object. Even a knife will work. Can you see it being forged? Or stamped out in a factory? Can you see the people making it?

The goal is to use scanning to focus your senses until you can see, hear, and feel the objects, origins, and memories. This type of exercise builds your visualization, awareness, sensing, scanning and focus, consciousness-shifting skills, and clairvoyance.

The trick is not to be afraid to let your imagination mix with the visualization. The skills used in this exercise are a precursor to pathworking and advanced psychic work.

IMAGINATION AS A SKILL

We are often told our imagination is a bad thing. Not so. Imagination is a great tool in the ways of Magic, Witchcraft, and psychism. Not letting our imagination flow restricts the other senses and visions we may otherwise receive. However, a word of caution.

Sometimes when practicing this, you may begin to feel anxious, uncomfortable, even scared. This is to be expected. These sensations occur because you are not used to shifting your consciousness, letting your imagination roam free, or recognizing how your body will respond to doing those things. The feeling is the same when we do any work that takes us to the edge of our comfort zone. Another caution: not everything our inner vision and imagination perceives is real and true.

Both of these are reasons why knowing yourself is so important in psychism. Scanning ourselves is the best way to tell the difference between what belongs to us, what is imagination, what is a real event, or if something belongs to someone else. Developing a practice of meditating on the event afterward is an excellent tool for clarity of what you have experienced.

MEDITATION EXPLAINED

I mention meditation a lot and with good reason. Meditation is a tool that brings mental clarity and increased focus. Meditation allows you the time and space to let go of your daily worries and shift your consciousness. Please do not let the idea of meditation scare you; there is no one right way to meditate.

Many people think that if you are not sitting cross-legged with an empty mind for hours you are not meditating. This is not so. You can be gardening, hiking, sewing, quietly sitting, or even allowing your mind to ramble and still be meditating. The trick is picking a method that suits you. There are books, apps, videos, and other information available to help you find a meditation you will enjoy.

Meditation is about the state your brain waves are in. The state of mind you are trying to achieve is called a theta state. The state of the brain waves is the marker of shifting your consciousness.

When I meditate, I light a candle as a light to guide me back. Lighting a candle to find my way back was something my mom taught me to ease my fears of getting lost. I also have a hard time keeping my eyes closed so I also put on a sleep mask. The mask provides deeper darkness with less distraction and improves my focus.

That is my way of meditating. Yours might be something very different. The outcome is important, not the how. The pause meditation is a good basic one to begin your practice.

The state the brain is in during meditation is much like when we are daydreaming or zoning out. Surprisingly, learning how to achieve that state at will is excellent for building skills used in meditation and psychism.

One of the topics mentioned in most texts on meditation is the monkey mind and getting that to stop. I have a different take on that. We have a monkey mind because our lives are so busy that our minds are not allowed to express themselves freely. While exploring that, I discovered that if I allowed my mind to just roam occasionally, later when I wanted it to quiet down it was not as difficult to accomplish. So I developed the simple wandering mind meditation.

Wandering Mind Meditation

Sit someplace comfortable and stare out a window, go for a walk, garden, or stare into a campfire. Turn off any music because listening to music or any other repetitive sound restricts the ability of the mind to roam freely and keeps you from paying attention to your thoughts. It is the practice of paying attention to our thoughts that makes this exercise effective.

Disciplined practice is important because it builds your skill to shift your consciousness at will. Once you practice meditation for a while you will be able to drop into a theta state with little effort.

Setting out a time each day is optimal. If you do not have that luxury, I recommend three times a week. At first, your meditation can be five minutes at a time then work your way up to an hour. It is best to keep a good meditation practice for the first two years. It takes roughly two years of regular meditation practice to train your brain to the level you need for advanced psychism.

Each time you meditate or do any of the exercises, you are stimulating certain neural synapses in your brain to connect to a new place they are not used to connecting to. During each practice, the neural synapse builds up muscle memory to that new connection. This makes it easier to get to this new mental place with just a thought the next time. Further, a good meditation and visualization practice will increase your ability to receive spontaneous conceptual information as you progress in your psychic and magical practices. Meditation aids in building intuition, self-trust, and trust in what you sense and what you see.

INTUITION EXPLAINED

It is important to know the difference between desire, imagination, and your intuition. A desire will feel different from intuition. A nudge from your intuition is often more physical rather than mental and each person's intuition presents in ways unique to the individual. I feel my intuition in my body first, then get an image of something after I pay attention to what stimulated my intuition.

Over time, I learned the difference between desire, whim, and true intuition. I accomplished that through scanning and self-knowledge, using self-scanning and journaling. Only you can tell the subtle differences between your wants and your intuition and keeping notes will help you keep track of the differences and prove them out.

Once when I was doing a tarot reading for a woman, a troublesome son kept appearing in the reading and nudging my intuition. I had to self-scan because I also had a troubled son at the time. I resisted mentioning him because I did not want my issues to bleed over. I could not determine what was mine and what was not, so I kept pushing it back. Yet the image came through repeatedly. I apologized and told her I had to mention something that was likely my issue so I could clear it from the reading by speaking it. When I did, it turned out her troublesome son was the very reason she was there.

Had I not been aware of my issues and read them to her as her own, I would have given a false reading, caused her undue worry, and ruined my reputation as a reader.

These things matter. When doing trance, ritual, aspecting, or anything that brings you to an edge mentally, you need to know what is you, what is spirit, and what is not you. You need to know how to adjust yourself appropriately and be able to push beyond your comfort zone in the moment effectively.

When asked suddenly to help with something, for example, you need to be able to push aside whatever is going on inside and find a way to get the job done. Not just in action and words, but in energy management. You need to be able to manage your emotions and quirks as you experience them in the moment. This requires quickly being able to note them and calm them while you proceed in action. I can say without a doubt that getting very skilled at the pause and scan has all but tamed my social anxiety, which has taught me the value of balance.

A PERSPECTIVE ON BALANCE

There are many ways to look at balance. First, you must realize that balance is not standing still in the center. It is ever moving, first one direction then another. How far it goes in any one direction is up to the circumstances and the choices made by the individual.

The key to balance is moving back to the center after having moved in a particular direction. Think of it like a pendulum. It remains still in the center until something makes it swing or move. Then when there is no more disturbance, it becomes centered once more. An entry from my journal shows an example of the meaning of balance.

2/5/18

While doing a pathworking with Odin, I was following him up the sharpest peak of a mountain. There was barely room for my foot on the path. Pebbles kept sliding out from under my feet making me slip while I was trying so hard to stay on the straight and narrow path. Then the pathworking suddenly changed to my following him up a peaked sand dune. Each time my foot stepped on the peak the sand would smash down so I was not able to walk a straight path. Then the scene changed to a place with a volcano in a land of ice. As the heat met the ice, it created mist. Odin turned to me and said, "Life is lived in the mists of chaos."

What I learned from this experience was that we all have challenging things in life that derail us from our chosen path. The things that derail us are the mists of chaos and where daily life is lived. It is choosing to swing back to center, i.e., balance, that keeps you on the path. It is then that the practice of joy and gratitude helps to ease the challenges of chaos as you strive to maintain your balance on your journey.

JOY

Having joy in your life brings emotional healing. I remember in the early days of my journey someone asked me to write about the things that brought me joy. At the time, I was at a loss; I did not even know the definition of the word.

Joy is the smallest thing that gives you pleasure, that makes you smile or laugh or eases your stress. For me, I was so deep into the drama and stress of my life that I had to actively seek something out every day that brought me joy. It began with me noticing that when the neighbor smiled at me or talked to me it made me feel better. Then I realized hearing the children play in the park across the street made me feel like I was not alone. I began to enjoy the sound of their playing. After I got my dog, joy was noticing how she wagged at me and played on the bed before I got up.

Because I chose to notice the joy and allow myself to feel it, it set my mood for the whole day. Through the exercise of writing down a joy for each day, I began to see my way back into life and out of depression and drama.

Through seeking out joy I began to see it was okay to claim good feelings for myself. It taught me it is not just the bad or upset feelings that we need to honor and validate for ourselves, but the good ones too. Coming to a place where you can say you deserve good feelings liberates you from other insecurities and fears that your beliefs fuel. Too often the drama in our lives or our obligations takes us to a place where we forget that we are entitled to feel the good feelings too. Some of us are so unfamiliar with good feelings we do not recognize them when they come, or they bring pain and fear with them.

To begin to heal, we must permit ourselves to feel good feelings and permit ourselves to have good moments with people. Start with the small stuff, such as a smile someone gives us, to demonstrate that we can experience joy and be safe when we do.

Joy Exercise

Go to a park or a busy street corner and notice the things that make you smile, such as the sun on your face, a child's laughter, or the color of a woman's dress. Notice the upbeat energy around you and absorb it, then journal about how you felt.

Once you are familiar with what joy is, you will want more. The more you pursue joy, the further away you will go from the negative. Pursuing joy will open the door to any emotional healing you need to do.

If you do not need emotional healing, becoming familiar with joy will allow you to know what it is when you pick it up from others.

GRATEFULNESS AND GRATITUDE

Next in spiritual evolution is gratefulness and gratitude, which are interchangeable. Have gratefulness for the joy, for the sense of healing, and gratitude for all the people who cross our paths in their many forms and ways. Gratefulness applies to all people, even the ones who frustrate you, those who make you angry or even harmed you. For some, this is a hard concept. Many ask how they can be grateful for what happened to them, when it was clearly wrong. In these cases when we grab on to being grateful, we survived, or were later proven correct and began our healing.

To be grateful to those who frustrate or challenge you takes you thanking them for showing you how much patience, tolerance, kindness, or even self-restraint you have. People in general mirror things back at you and sometimes that image is not flattering, but it is still yours to deal with. The people who frustrate you give you the opportunity to see areas in which you need more work.

One of the ways I practice gratefulness toward all is when I am driving. Maybe there is a slow driver who is frustrating me. To apply gratefulness, I think of how grateful I am this slow driver is keeping me from getting a speeding ticket. In the beginning, most of my gratefulness was expressed through a clenched jaw and accompanied by my grumbling "gee thanks," but I was still grateful to the person for shedding light on things. The "gee thanks" attitude is the faking-it-till-you-make-it type of work we often encounter on our journey into gratitude.

I have seen gratitude transform many people's lives. I have seen faces change from being harsh to being soft. I have seen hard-core shields let down and replaced by a genuinely loving person. I have seen gratitude change a person from tears and anger to love and laughter. I have also seen people who were stuck in the unproductive cycle of their drama heal and move on. Seeing all this gave me the power of gratitude to heal lives.

Gratitude Exercise

As you go through your day, seek out things to be grateful for. It can be your job, your friends and family, your pets, or your plants, pretty much anything in the beginning. This first step gets you familiar with practicing gratitude.

Once you are practiced at being grateful for your blessings and the good things in your life, begin a practice of being grateful for the things that challenge or frustrate you—it eases them greatly. To do this, write those challenging things down in your journal. Include your feelings about them and explore why they are difficult; reflect on how gratitude can heal them or change your perspective about them. This will require you to be willing rather than willful, which is a challenge by itself.

Chapter 2
EFFECTS OF SOCIAL CONDITIONING

Over the years of working with people in social services, I discovered that many folks, myself included, often had stuff they were not even aware of getting in the way of their desired progress. Many of us spend years trying to get that stuff in check. This also applied when I became a Pagan teacher. I found students so twisted up about life issues they could not move on and learn new ways. I saw this in folks who were trying to build a spiritual life as well.

Many of the things people struggle with fall under the category of spiritual evolution. In my work, I have narrowed spiritual evolution down to several components that the majority of people experience as they begin their spiritual journey.

Most people choose a spiritual path and then try to change themselves to fit that path, leaving many to have poor experiences. When I researched this, my conclusion was that a person needs to get in touch with their deeper self, be comfortable and confident with who they are, then choose a spiritual path that fits that internal part of them. Not the other way around. When I began applying this concept to the way I taught Paganism, I saw my students have greater success, and greater spiritual satisfaction.

To get in touch with your deeper self and confidence, you have to look at who you are now and what you think and believe now. In effect, you build a new foundation based on who you really are at the core. A psychic needs to know what belongs to them and what does not, what influences them, and how they typically respond to those influences.

Now you may be thinking, *Isn't this a book on psychism? Why do I need this mumbo jumbo?* Well, because being on a path of spiritual evolution is needed for psychics to be mentally sound and spiritually strong when they encounter many of the things they do. It is also of great benefit in Magic and Witchcraft. I recommend reading through the entire book to get a good grip on what it presents. Then come back to the parts you feel you need more work on. If you read a chapter and find you do not need what is presented, wonderful, but you now have a manual to help others who may need it.

In this chapter, you will look at your beliefs about the world, yourself, and others. Psychics need self-knowledge to be effective. Self-knowledge clears a path to the necessary skills and keeps the information received clear, which is the goal of doing this work, but where to start? You begin by looking at how your current beliefs were formed, which we all get through some form of social conditioning from outside influences.

SOCIAL CONDITIONING: WHAT IS IT?

As we grow up, many outside influences teach us, guide us, and tell us what to do or believe. A big chunk of this information is about how to manage life and stay safe as we grow. The rest is given to us by others based on their experiences, their beliefs, and their opinions. We then blend all of this input with our own ideas. We rarely question that social conditioning as we grow, yet that early conditioning still influences us greatly.

Many people struggle with making things work the way they were told they are supposed to work. Some are left feeling inadequate, broken, or incapable. They may feel they are to blame for things not working. This happens when you try to make things work in ways that work for others but are not right for you. Doing that can get you caught in an unproductive cycle.

Looking at your social conditioning and beliefs can break those cycles. Examining your conditioning gives you knowledge about how and why things affect you as they do. This work increases self-confidence and independence. You also get an in-depth look at how you have been living your life and why. All of this gives you the power of choice and control over your life.

Social Conditioning Exercise, Part 1

Write about the ways you have been socially conditioned, including what you were taught about money, relationships, and how you should live. Keep entries short, more like a list, without looking at them too deeply for now.

Next, write down what you would change. Write from the perspective of "If I had no restrictions or limits, this is what I would do differently with money, relationships, my life, etc." Pretend there is nothing that would block you from making those changes. Let it flow right from the heart and soul. This can take some time, so be gentle with yourself. When you are done writing, read it again. Think about it for a week. Talk it out with your friends and family or another support person.

Social Conditioning Exercise, Part 2

Write what is not working for you. Then for the next week think about how you can make the not-working work. How can you make those changes happen? Even very small things can bring big changes over time. Let your imagination and visualization roam wild! Do not let any blocks stop your thinking.

At the end of the week, write what you *now* think about what is working and what is not. Look back on this work often for clarity and inspiration.

SELF-TAPES: OUR MENTAL CRITIC

Self-tapes are what we tell ourselves in our minds. Self-tapes are the thoughts in our minds that call us names such as stupid, dumbass, air brained, and so much more. Social conditioning creates these thoughts and our insecurities fuel them.

These tapes eventually become what we believe about ourselves deep down. Changing these tapes increases confidence and changes how we feel about ourselves. Changing them can be done through pivoting (more on pivoting later).

Self-Tape Exercise

Pay attention to what you say to yourself. In the moments when you call yourself silly, clumsy, dumb, and so on, stop and take a moment to tell yourself those things are not true. Set a goal to stop telling yourself those things and continue working toward that.

EGO: OUR MENTAL PROTECTOR

The ego uses self-tapes such as "You should not do that," "What are you thinking?" and "What if?" The ego uses these tapes to preserve the self. It will also use emotions such as anger, judgment, blame, fear, doubt, defensiveness, and more for preservation. The ego uses mostly emotion that is seldom fact.

I have heard many enlightened people say we need to get rid of our ego entirely. I disagree because we are, after all, human, and humans have egos; it is just part of who we are.

I could write a whole book about the ego, but Eckhart Tolle beat me to it with his book *The Power of Now*. Tolle talks about our egoic mind and its effect on our lives. He believes that as long as we give our ego free rein, we will never truly be at ease with ourselves or our lives except momentarily when we get something we think we want.

The ego is a derived sense of self and needs external things to soothe it, such as your work, social status, education, appearance, and relationships, none of which are the real you. The person you are in your heart and soul is the real you. Social conditioning plays on these parts of the ego to make us believe those external things are what we need to function and be productive. This only makes it harder to deal with the ego and its effect on our life.

Once we understand the dynamics of ego paired with social conditioning and how that drives us, we can begin to turn it into something more positive in our lives.

FAKE IT TILL YOU MAKE IT: A MAGICAL ACT

To change or adapt self-tapes, you need to rewire the synapses of your brain and that process begins with pivoting. Pivoting takes you from something negative to something positive over and over until the more positive place is your default place.

The first stage of pivoting is faking it till you make it. During this stage, many feel they are being fake or not being their true selves. That is true, and it is normal. You are not being your *old* self you are being someone *new* so it feels fake.

That feeling of being fake is the ego challenging you. Because the ego fears change, it can be a battle. Faking it till you make it and acting as if are the tools used as you create a new you, and they are a magical act, because you are manifesting a new you! So be diligent yet gentle with yourself. The example from my journal further explains what this process is like.

3/14/13

I feel like I am faking it and I am dealing with lessons on judgment and attachments and trying to let all that go. I find it surprising when I compare what I say my beliefs are to what I am putting forward. When I see the gaps, the contrast is stark. It makes all kinds of doubts rise. I wonder if I am all I say I am, and sometimes I feel like a fake, then I begin to fear I really am a fake. I had to talk it out with my husband. He has helped me to understand that what I am feeling is just the process of change. To get through it I have had to explore the ego thing with more depth. In doing so I discovered my fear of being fake was my ego wanting me to stay safely where I was and not take risks by growing. This tells me that those doubts are part of my transition as I emerged into what I am becoming and want to be.

This journal entry shows what it is like to deal with the fear of change and being on the threshold of that change. I now know that in transition, we fake it till we make it. We step past the threshold and fully into the change, and that process takes us out of our comfort zone. It is interesting how faking it till I made it created confidence and trust in myself once I was on the other side of the process. Part of faking it till you make it uses the tool of pivoting.

THE PIVOTING SKILL

To pivot, you first must catch yourself thinking something you do not want to be thinking, such as *I am a fake*. When you stop that thought and turn your thoughts to something constructive, you have successfully pivoted. The constructive thought can be anything pleasant or informative: a color, a dress, a roof, a car, a nice memory, the sunshine, something you want to learn or remember, or even bunny rabbits.

Pivoting includes finding your mind or emotions in a space you do not want them to be in and stopping to find something positive or pleasant to focus on until the less desired thoughts pass. Sometimes when things were intense, I would mentally and obsessively repeat a song I remembered until the moment past and I could move on. Pivoting can help when you are angry, in an emotional state, or when you are being negative or judgmental.

Pivoting breaks the thought process. It interrupts the connection to the synapse the brain uses to get to the undesired thought and redirects it to a different synapse. By doing this over and over, the brain gets used to the more positive synapse and eventually will seek out the positive synapse instead of the negative one. Pivoting works in changing many undesired behaviors. Pivoting also helps in changing your perspective.

Does this mean you will never have another negative thought? No! But you will recognize what to do when they occur. They will be more manageable, less frequent, and less intense. Once you have a fair grip on pivoting, you will begin to relax about things that used to bother you and you will start to trust yourself more.

Pivoting Example

I remember a day I spent at the DMV shortly after I had begun the pivot exercises. I had been there for a long time. I had been directed to several agents and was seeing yet another one. She was requesting I pay a fee that happened to be all the money I had managed to put in my savings. I was crushed and angry. When I became aware of myself, I felt my fists were tight, my face was flushed, and I was ready to lash out.

At that moment, I remembered to pivot. I paused, took a breath, and began to tell myself that this person was only doing their job, and the rules and regulations are not their fault. I began to get calmer, my fists unclenched, and I took another deep breath. With the anger and emotions now calmed, I was able to choose how to act instead of being led by my emotions. Calmly, I finished my transaction and left feeling much better about myself. I was still upset, but I dealt with that appropriately once I was home.

After such an event, journaling helps to process the feeling fully. This lets you learn from the experience. It is self-nurturing, allowing healthy venting and release.

Will you be perfect at it every time? No. Will it work every time? No. But you will get better at it, and it will get easier. Sometimes in order to pivot I have to coach my breathing and focus on the facts until things calm down. Focusing on the facts is another part of pivoting and is very effective, and it is often what I am doing in my moments of pause.

To focus on the facts, ask yourself if this feeling is real, and if it is reasonable that you are feeling like this. Think about whether you are feeling what others around you are feeling or if they are your feelings. Consider if you are safe and if this feeling is just an impulse. As you consider these things, coach yourself as you focus on your breathing. Throughout this process, it is important to trust yourself.

Pivoting Exercise

For one week, whenever you have negative thoughts, an upsetting moment, or thoughts you want to change, take a breath, think, then turn your thoughts to something positive, constructive, or enjoyable.

Practice as often as possible. Write about it in your journal to help you. This work teaches you to trust yourself as you gain control and confidence in yourself.

TRUSTING YOURSELF AND SELF-TAPES

Ever hear the phrase "It is much easier to trust a stranger than it is to trust yourself"? This is true because there is less risk involved in trusting a stranger than yourself. This is especially true if you have been taught through social conditioning to doubt yourself and that doubt is reinforced by self-tapes that keep running in your head. Self-tapes are the voice inside your head that echoes doubt, fear, ego, and your beliefs about yourself. They play a big part in how you trust yourself.

For example, my self-tapes told me I was stupid, less than average in intelligence, and incompetent. I felt this way about myself even though I had completed college with a 4.0 grade average, was Phi Theta Kappa, and on the dean's list. I was a homeowner and a counselor. I was trying so hard to prove the tapes wrong by making life outside myself perfect, which takes a huge amount of time and energy, I might add. All of this demonstrates how social conditioning and self-tapes often affect our lives.

Looking at the facts instead of believing the self-tapes is how we prove the tapes wrong. However, you must accept and believe that the facts are true to make this work. It can be difficult to allow ourselves to feel and believe the good stuff but that is what frees us from this kind of misery when we experience it. You can change the self-tapes with the pivoting skill.

How does this apply to psychism, Witchcraft, and Magic? Well, it is hard to be a competent tarot reader when you doubt yourself. It is difficult to lead a ritual when you doubt your every move. It is difficult to be convincing when petitioning a deity if you doubt yourself. If you doubt you, then it is likely others will too, which makes it harder to accomplish your magical goals.

Trusting Yourself Exercise, Part 1

In your journal, write down all the things you have accomplished. They can be simple things such as *I get up each day and . . . , I go to school or work every day, I got a promotion, I care for my family.* Go back as far as you can remember with the things you have accomplished.

As you reflect on your accomplishments, let them sink in, accept they are really you, and allow yourself to feel good about them.

This is healthy self-nurturing and giving yourself credit where credit is due. One of the things I have learned over the years is that if you wait for others to give you credit where it is due or to notice your accomplishments, not only will you constantly be disappointed, but you will constantly give your personal power away and keep the cycle of doubt going. Nurturing ourselves breaks this cycle.

Trusting Yourself Exercise, Part 2

In the morning, read aloud one of your accomplishments. Choose a new one each day until you have gotten through them all. Each day, tell yourself *I accomplished this, and it is okay to feel good about it.*

This teaches you what it feels like to accept the good in you. This builds confidence in the mind, and belief will soon follow. The idea here is to focus on the good stuff and leave the rest behind for now. This also trains your mind for later use in magical practices. Once you begin to trust yourself more you begin to notice things you need to let go of too.

LETTING GO

To leave the undesired behind in this framework is called letting go. Letting go is the art form of exercising choice deliberately, which is a paradox because letting go gives us control and freedom. Learning to let go increases your ability to focus your mind at will, aiding you in dreamwork, trance spells, and ritual work.

I often call letting go an art form because it requires choice, focus, and purpose. We have all heard the phrase "Learn to pick your battles." That phrase is at the heart of letting go. There are some confusing things in letting go. For example, the most common misunderstanding is that if you let go you stop caring. This is not true. It is possible to care and still let others experience their own journey and consequences. This means we are only in control of ourselves, not what others do or say, and we have to let go of those attachments. When we let others experience their own consequences, it is a greater act of love and compassion because we are giving them the space to live their own lives their own way, without judgment or blame.

We do this while we focus on making the best of ourselves. It is a way of being supportive but not fixing another person's life. Letting go includes our past and forgiving ourselves for our past and doing that for others too. It can be like walking a tightrope as you carefully navigate the path of letting go.

My journey to letting go was a long one because I had to face surrender, which is part of the spiritual evolution process. You may fear or fight surrender (I sure did) but surrendering to the truth of yourself and your life is the first step in moving forward into letting go and forgiveness. The amazing thing I discovered is that once I did surrender, I gained clarity about who I was and wanted to be. I gained control of my life and it felt like freedom. I felt like I had broken the chains of my unproductive cycles. I realized I had let toxic people into my life, and I had to be willing to let them go.

It took courage to cut them out of my life and some of them were family. To my surprise, when I let them go, my stress was drastically reduced and my overall health began to improve. With my self-confidence and emotions now mostly in check, I began to make choices about how I was feeling, to think first then act rather than being driven by instant reaction or being ruled by my emotions.

A vital part of this work is letting go of the past since it does not serve us well to continue living in the past. We only move forward by not letting it define us. Letting go of the past allows us to begin living in the present, moment by moment. This takes practice and is hard. It takes making what you want for your life an important goal and rediscovering what is important to you, and it may require you to get to know yourself again.

It also requires you to be willing rather than willful to clean the slate and let go of it all.

But what you get in return for letting go is peace of mind, self-confidence, a restored belief system, a sense of self, self-respect, a sense of accomplishment, and independence. Once that work is complete, you will have a solid foundation to operate from, and you can do whatever is within your grasp.

SPIRITUAL LETTING GO

How we let go spiritually is different from how we let go in everyday life. Letting go in spirituality is when we let go of a part of ourselves and tune in to what is beyond what our eyes can see. This helps us explore intuition, threshold work, stepping aside, and so much more. Magically, we let go when we send off our intentions and magical acts. We let go and let in when we read cards. We let go when we meditate, when we do rituals and many other things in Magic and spirituality. It is a skill many of us use but are often not aware of. When we use letting go with awareness and learn it well, it becomes a tool that is consciously at our disposal anytime, which increases our spiritual, magical, and psychic effectiveness.

Have you ever thought about how you let go spiritually? Worship, prayer, and veneration are the most common ways. When you pray, worship, or venerate a deity, you let go of thoughts of the daily world. You pivot to thoughts only of the deity or spirit of choice. Your personality and ego are put aside for the moment, and you release yourself to the work at hand. This is letting go spiritually. The same is true when you listen to your "gut feeling," your intuition, or your higher self. When you listen to your spirit guides, you let go by putting your ego and personality aside.

This skill set is used in all forms of the psychic and spiritual processes. The action is consciously shifting your consciousness and focus is the end result. You can achieve this change in consciousness using pause, sensing, pivoting, and letting go.

Consciously shifting the consciousness is putting yourself in an altered state of mind. When you do this, you put your ego and personality aside to listen and focus. This is where Magic happens. You let go because you trust the process. You have no fear of it because you know it well from the practice you do. However, any fear can block the whole process of letting go as described earlier. So if this exercise does not work for you, try looking at some of your fears around letting go spiritually. Do you fear losing yourself? Do you fear something bad coming in? Do you still fear not being good enough or that you cannot control what is going on? Hint: You are not supposed to always control what is going on spiritually; that is the whole point of letting go. Trust the process, trust yourself, and let go.

Spiritual Letting Go Exercise

Write in your journal about what letting go spiritually means to you. List ways that you let go. Then contemplate or meditate on it for a week. Get to know how and why you use the skill. Elaborate on the details so it can become a tool you can use consciously.

Letting go is important to developing your intuition. Letting go helps to remove any blocks you may have in developing your intuition, which is the next level we will explore. So practice pivoting, letting go, and shifting your consciousness to prepare for developing your intuition.

Chapter 3
DEVELOPING INTUITIVE SKILLS

There are many parts to intuition, which is usually referred to as our gut instincts or as listening to that voice inside. Some define intuition as opening our minds and bodies to the vibrations of the unseen, and unheard, which is another vague description of tapping into your intuition. My goal is to provide a step-by-step process on how to connect to and use intuition. To do this, I had to look at my own intuition and break down the process. I discovered intuition begins with what I call the five faculties of the mind: perception, reason, intellect, discernment, and will.

FIVE FACULTIES OF THE MIND

To know and be aware of how we use these five faculties of the mind plays an important role in psychism. We use these functions without thought many times a day, but once you begin to use them as tools toward your psychic skills, they improve your skills and mental clarity.

Perception

Perception, the first of the five faculties of the mind, is a concept or idea that you have. The perception I speak of here is different than the perception I spoke of in the first chapter. Here we use perception as a magical tool. To use perception as a tool you apply your intellect to it. Then with intellect, you ask yourself *What do I know about this thing I have perceived?* When the five faculties of our mind are used as a tool, it sends a signal, usually to the body. That signal is the "gut feeling" or perception that there is something we need to pay attention to.

Perception is the foundation for everything in the mind. Without perception, we would not have discernment, intellect, or reason. What would there be to apply those things to if we first did not have a perception or idea of something? We interpret our dreams based on our perceptions, and we react to everything based on our perceptions of them.

Perception gives us everything our minds contain. You can have a perception of something without having or using intellect. But you cannot apply intellect to something without first having a perception. You cannot work psychism, Magic, and Witchcraft without perception. Your everyday perception of the world keeps you safe and helps you relate to others and be a viable person in society. Your perception used as a spiritual tool helps you see this spiritual reality. Your spiritual perception is unique to you. Only you know what it means for you to dream of a house or dog. This kind of perception is more mutable than normal perceptions, meaning it can be changed easily. The tools you use for changing your perception are pivoting, awareness, and the five faculties of the mind.

Reason

In the five faculties of the mind, reason comes after perception. In reason, you ask yourself how this perception makes sense and if it is reasonable. In spirituality, reason is the cause or motive for your belief and gives you a premise to support the belief.

In spirituality, you must use reason with caution. Reason is a logical function tied to ego and social conditioning. It can reason you right out of your spiritual beliefs if you are not careful. Therefore, applying awareness to the five faculties of the mind is an important function. The following journal entry is an experience I had that demonstrates how tricky reason can be.

4/12/14

I was hosting a public event at my home and posted my address on social media. Five hours before the event, a man came to my door asking about it. The moment I saw him I was filled with unreasonable fear and began to tremble and panic. The man's appearance gave me no reason to fear him but I was overwhelmed with fear. As my mind began to work, I used my pivoting and pause skills to calm myself and told him to come back later. He did come back and while he was there all of us were uneasy and uncomfortable. My feelings were so intense they were difficult to quickly sort out in the moment. My reason told me there was no reason to fear him initially. My intellect then said, if it is not reasonable to fear him, it must be your issue to sort out, so put it aside. But that horrible gut feeling remained, which told me something was wrong.

I had people in my home waiting for me. I had to let go and set it aside until such a time I could address it. My intuition had worked correctly the moment I opened the door. But in the primal moment of fear, social conditioning and the five faculties of the mind reverted to their linear functions, and reason caused me not to trust myself and to doubt what I felt was real. Later, we discovered he was a very scary person and was wanted by the law. I made sure to tell him not to come back and we all felt lucky it went as well as it did.

Intellect

Intellect follows reason in the five faculties. We use intellect when we apply what we know toward something and examine how it functions. We ask ourselves what we know about this thing. What have I learned from experience about this thing? What have others told me about this? And we apply that to the perception and reason. As we apply awareness to intellect, it assists us in making a choice about it.

Discernment

Discernment is next in the five faculties. Discernment shows us the difference between what we believe and what is social conditioning. Discernment is where we consider how a concept or idea fits into our beliefs and intellect and further assists in making a choice. Discernment is followed by your will.

Will

Will is where you put something into action with speech, writing, or other action. Using your will is an act of Magic. Will is the mental effort used to affect an outcome by the use of desire and thought. It is often confused with intention. Saying "I intend for this to occur" is much less powerful than saying "By my will so mote it be."

As an exercise, stand in front of a mirror and say, "My intention is to have _____ occur." Notice how it makes you feel emotionally and physically. Then shake it off, take a break, then come back to the mirror and say, "By my will so mote it be" and notice the difference in how you feel. Words are power and energy, and words can make Magic happen.

Your will is the power of your mind driven by the soul's desire. Will drives your determination, keeps you on your goal, and helps you to create the life you want to live. To believe you have power is not a bad thing as you have been led to believe in today's society.

Not being afraid to speak directly about having personal power is one of the things I find most common in successful practitioners. It serves to build confidence and skill and adds power to the work, which is why I recommend changing the words you use on a daily basis from the passive to the confident. For example, you might say, "I would like to do that." Change it to "I will do that." Changing these speech patterns creates big changes in your demeanor and thought process that will carry over to your psychic skills, your Magic, and your belief about yourself and will breed confidence and trust in yourself.

The Five Faculties Exercise

Each week for five weeks in a row, pick a different faculty of the mind to focus on. Note when you are using it and what it feels like.

For perception, keep a number tally of the times you use perception instead of writing out each event. The goal here is to become aware of when you use perception or another faculty of the mind until you know how each one feels when they arise.

On a side note, intellect and reason can be hard to separate in our thought process. Reason is what is reasonable as it applies to what we know of something intellectually. Applying discrimination is where you may agree with reason but choose to modify it in some way.

The goal is to draw them out to become tools in Magic and psychism. Particularly note any psychic stimuli that occurs during this exercise.

THE INTUITION SKILL

The culmination of the five faculties of the mind is what you perceive as intuition. Your mind translates perceptions and images into what you can conceptualize, but we must ask if what we conceptualize is reality, a mere concept of the imagination, or fantasy? This is important and to discover this, you apply reason to the thought process, then add awareness with the five faculties, which opens the door to your higher self. This skill building creates the ability to recognize information impressed on us as non-thoughts in the mind. This action then triggers our subconscious and superconscious minds to transmit information to the conscious mind for interpretation and signals our body and is called our intuition.

Intuition is an instinctual, primal force within us all. We use intuition when we are young to figure out the world. As an adult, you only need to draw it out and apply your awareness to it. Remember how you used it when you were young. So the first step is to sit down, reflect on how you used intuition before, and journal.

Everyone uses one of two types of intuition without noticing every day. One type is the intuition you use for basic survival and getting through the day. This is the intuition used by your daily conscious mind, much like a sidewalk you walk down every day and never notice.

The other type of intuition is the inner intuition. The inner intuition is that sense of what resides within you. It is your inner knowledge. This is the intuition you typically get conditioned out of. This is the one that you often brush aside as coincidence and fail to validate.

Intuition can reveal a whole new world to you. It can help you pick a partner, find a job, keep you in touch with others, and keep you in touch with the beyond. With applied awareness and the use of the five faculties, intuition can be built into a useful tool. Intuitions allow you to get a clearer picture of what is going on, which makes it so you can easily move through the moment fully informed. You cultivate and strengthen intuition and awareness by paying closer attention to whole-body responses to information, people, and situations.

Your body will tell you what you need to know. Do you get a tingling in the scalp every time you have an intuitive moment? Or a feeling in your stomach? Do you feel pain in some part of your body when you are about to do something? These are the kinds of body clues you can get when your intuition is active.

Intuition does not start in the body, however; it starts in the physical reaction we feel. It is the body reacting to what the mind is telling it. We humans just do not seem to notice it until the body tells us. That is where the phrase "gut reaction" comes from. The more we apply awareness, which we get from using the pause and scan, and the five faculties of the mind to these body responses, the more we build our skill.

Once while driving through town on an errand, I got a nudge from my intuition to go into a Christian thrift store. I really did not want to, but my intuition, which sometimes feels like an impulse, pushed me, so I went. When I got to the counter, the woman behind the counter mentioned my pentacle necklace. I asked if she knew what it meant, she looked over her shoulder and said yes. I discreetly gave her my business card and told her if she ever wanted to chat to hit me up. She gasped and said, "I have been looking for a Pagan group here for so long I did not think there were any!" Later she joined our group.

Intuition Exercise 1

For one week, no matter where or when you are, apply your awareness, pause, and scan to notice all the little aches and twinges your body is experiencing. Then apply the five faculties of the mind to them. What is the body wanting you to pay attention to? If you see nothing before you with your eyes, scan inward. If nothing is going on for you, scan those around you. Write about the experience in your journal as soon as you can.

The body may be telling you not to go into that meeting. It might be sending you signals about the person you are about to meet. It may be telling you something is wrong and to use caution. It can also be sending you good signals, such as the meeting will be great, the person may be great, and so on. It can tell you if you should send that resume and much more. With practice, your intuition and intellect can work well together to provide great insights on how to improve your life.

I share this because it demonstrates that none of us are perfect. It shows why building trust in yourself, building your intuition, and having a relationship with intuition and intellect is key.

There is a dance between fear and trust in us all. Yes, we must respect the intelligence of our analytical minds, yet as psychics, we know there is a time and place for our minds to be used. In the moment there is a deeper wisdom to guide you. It is your choice of which one you will listen to.

All of this highlights that intuition is multidimensional. Intuition goes beyond what can be seen with our eyes and offers solutions that the everyday mind alone cannot appreciate. Intuition is why the phrase "You have the answers within" is true. The following exercise is excellent for developing this level of intuition.

Intuition Exercise 2

Go to a park, a city square, a library, a bookstore, a hospital lobby, anywhere that is typically busy with people. Find a comfortable spot to sit where you will not be disturbed by anyone and turn off your phone.

Begin with the pause meditation. Once in a meditative state, expand your scan and begin to sense and feel the space around you. Then apply your inner intuition or just your senses to further scan the space around you. Then further expand your senses out to scan the people nearby. Stay with that for a moment and just sense their presence and movement.

Once you have that down, begin scanning and sensing the emotions or thoughts you can pick up from the people or the general mood of the area. Then gently open your eyes. Slowly look around to see if what you felt matches what you see; stay with it for a moment. With eyes open, look at a person and see if you can still sense them.

With this exercise, it is important not to let your eyes do the telling. The goal is not to rely only on your eyes but to rely on your inner vision, and intuition. When you are done, journal about your experience. Doing this at every opportunity will greatly increase your skill level and, eventually, you will be able to do this with just a thought.

SEEING AS A SKILL

What our eyes see can either trigger the use of our intuition or lead us away from it. We read body language regularly, usually without realizing it. However, when we visually read that body language and apply intuition to it also, we get insight into what is occurring that our eyes cannot see.

For example, I can glance up and see a homeless person and simply note they are there, or I can let my gaze linger a bit longer and notice details. Are they wearing shoes? Does their appearance tell me they are very desperate or a danger? As I do this, my intuition kicks in and tells me empathically the deeper story of what they are experiencing. This type of sight is explained further in the following journal entry.

3/2/18

I was in a restaurant having lunch when I heard the waitress being rude to a homeless man who only had a cup of coffee. When she came to my table, I told her I would like to buy the man breakfast. She rudely replied, "He had breakfast, he is just lingering and being obnoxious." She walked away before I could reply. She went to a table behind me and bad-mouthed the homeless man even more. I watched and studied the homeless man. I could only see him from one side.

Using all my senses I began to get the feeling he was in distress and something was very wrong. He stood up to leave and stumbled; from across the room the waitress loudly said, "You are drunk and need to leave!" I got up to assist him. When I got close to him, I noticed an acrid sweet smell coming from him. He was pale and sweating as he looked at me then passed out. The waitress wanted to call the cops and have him removed.

I told her to call 911 because the man was diabetic and crashing. It turned out I was right. Because of my prior experiences with diabetics, the sweet acrid smell, his sweating, and his passing out were all I needed to know.

If I had not used my other senses to tell me something was wrong before I approached him, I would not have been there to get him medical help. I would have simply left the restaurant because I was uncomfortable with the waitress. Our senses, if combined and applied, can tell us a great many things that our eyes fail to.

There are many ways to see and our intuition is a big part of that, but not the only one. Sometimes if we look deep enough, we can see the energy waves around us, colors, or auras.

SYNCHRONICITY

Synchronicity is also a way of seeing. Synchronicity is how the universe, the world, and the beyond speak to us. I traced *synchronicity* as far back as 1889. It is defined as the coincidental occurrence of events, especially psychic events such as similar thoughts in widely separated people. These occurrences seem related but are not explained by conventional means of causality. In the 1920s, Carl Jung described it as two or more unrelated random events that happen within a short period of time that come to have a significant meaning.

Jung believed that synchronicity was more than just an intellectual exercise and could be part of a spiritual awakening. Further, he believed, synchronicity shared similar characteristics to the intervention of grace and has a role in our lives like that of dreams. (More on Jung's thoughts can be found in *Synchronicity: An Acasual Connecting Principle.*) Many think synchronicity is just coincidences. When I read all the signs, such as in the journal entry above, it helps me with manifesting my desires and helping others. Because in my life there are rarely coincidences.

Has something ever come up a couple of times, separate from each other, and you wondered how odd that is? Such as an old friend's name appearing several times in different ways over a week, only for it to lead you to call them. In that call, you find out something is going on. Or a topic or item pops up in the same manner that gets you thinking about it in some deeper way?

It happens to everyone sooner or later. A certain number pop up wherever you go; an old friend you haven't seen in twenty years or since high school appears the same day you're looking at their picture in a yearbook, or you are singing a song and turn on the radio and the same song is playing.

Synchronicity is seeing signs of the universe around you that would otherwise go unnoticed. I think of this as the universe, world, or spirit directly speaking to me. Now, does everything have significant meaning? No, sometimes finding a white feather is just a gift from nature, and sometimes what we think is an intuitive nudge is simply impulse or stress.

It is these variables that make the pause, scan, and the five faculties of the mind valuable in determining the meaning of our perceptions. Keep in mind there are no perfect answers so be gentle with yourself. We are, after all, human and fallible.

Paying attention to synchronicity daily can become a way of living. It is a process that takes time. Sometimes you will be wrong and sometimes you will not. Practice will increase your accuracy rate. Journaling will help you track your progress and show you where you need more work.

Synchronicity Exercise

For one month, keep track of anything you think is a coincidence or other odd things that stand out. Note anything additional that may relate when it catches your attention. When you have such an occurrence, apply your intuition and pause and scan skills to it to look for a deeper meaning that needs attention. Synchronicity plays a big part in helping others and with staying in the flow of the universe. Synchronicity also plays a part in creating the lives we want, which is called cocreation. To cocreate you will need the skill of manifesting.

USING MANIFESTING TO CREATE

To manifest you need to determine what in your life is not working for you and give yourself permission to change it. Then clearly decide what you do want to have or create. Being clear on what you want and permitting yourself to change can be the hard part but is vital to the process. I suggest journaling or meditating to get clear about what you want and need.

Giving yourself permission to change requires the belief that it is okay to do so. Being clear on what you want requires searching beyond your surface whims and impulses. The axiom "Be careful what you ask for" very much applies here. You can and do get what you ask for because manifesting works and the universe responds.

We create with manifesting, and it can be anything for anyone. In my journey, I discovered I had been socially conditioned that it was not okay to do good things for myself. I discovered it was difficult to break such habits and beliefs that had been learned over time. To break the idea of "I had to do what I was told," I had to become the adult in my mind and give myself permission to make changes as I desired, unbound by prior influences.

Nature abhors a vacuum and will fill it for you if you do not. This is a magical principle. I consider it a law of Magic. The biggest example of this I know of is when the universe has seen fit to take everything from a person. It has happened to me and maybe you too and it is a heck of an unexpected ride. However, if and when you choose to fill the vacuum or empty space in your life yourself, you can choose what you like and what you want in your life.

As you create your life, it will have you questioning beliefs like "you have to have a nine-to-five job or go to school." To a degree that is true, but it does not have to be your entire life or the only thing you do. Nor do you have to do those things in the same way everyone else does. You can allow yourself to be as creative about things as you want.

For manifesting skills, you must believe that the job or school is only a means to an end. The job and school are only the vehicle to get where you want to be. They do not have to be what you solely identify as, or what you are forever. The reason for this is because you must hold manifestation loosely so the universe has room to flow through your life. The same is true of money. We have to give money room to flow through our lives. If we hold on too tight to it, there will be no flow. To experience this kind of flow, try the following exercise.

Manifesting Exercise, Part 1

Get with another person or a group of people and find an item that is very important to you. Hold the important item and think about how valuable it is to you and hold it dearly. While you are full of those feelings, offer the item to the other person and say, "I freely give this to you," and hand it to them. Once they take it, notice how you feel; you should feel space, a type of release. That space is the vacuum which triggers the universe to fill it like water filling a hole. This means the more you let things flow through your life, the more things come into your life. That is the basic principle of manifesting. The flow and manifesting work best if you remain open to any possibility, rather than holding on to strict ideas and rules about how things are to happen.

Manifesting Exercise, Part 2

Write down all the wants that come to mind, even the silly stuff. If it comes to mind that you want to raise bunnies, write it down. If it comes to you that you would like to know more about world religions, write it down. This is the first level of wants. Look over them, and circle one or two that seem important, and set them aside.

Manifesting Exercise, Part 3

For this deeper level, go as far back in your memory as you can. Write down every idea you can remember of what you wanted to be or had an interest in. You may have to rack your brain or meditate or use visualization but keep writing.

When you are done, circle several that seem the most appealing or important to you and set them aside.

Manifesting Exercise, Part 4

Write down every great idea, invention, political solution, world-changing idea, healing, or spiritual idea you ever thought of. Is there a topic or activity popping up? When you are done, look at your lists. Is there a pattern emerging or a group of similar things? Is there a general theme to what you have written? These topics and themes give you an idea of what kind of work or creative ventures you would enjoy.

Manifesting Exercise, Part 5

Write about the topics or activities that you circled. How do you feel about them now? Are there things you want in your life? Explore unusual ways, and ways you may never have thought of to help you accomplish them. Write out your goals and make a plan. Start with small steps. Then keep it in the back of your mind as you go through your daily life.

Keeping your goals and plans in the back of your mind allows your intuition and synchronicity to work for you by presenting you with unusual and spontaneous opportunities. You may walk into a store one day and find what you want on sale.

By now you may be asking, how does cocreation of my regular life relate to psychism and Magic? Simply put, mastering cocreation builds first-level skills that you will use as you develop your psychic and magical skills.

SPIRITUAL CREATION

Manifesting and creating your life includes your spiritual life. You have been created by some means, and part of that "Creator" resides within you. This means that in your own way you are a creator too. Not all creation is in the hands of deity or some power outside of us. That is something we have been led to believe through social conditioning. Otherwise, manifesting would not be possible, and it is.

We have the power of creation but have never been given the idea or permission to fully explore it and use it. For myself, I eventually broke the rules of my social conditioning and created a spiritual life that openly included my own spirituality in a unique way and you can too, if that is your desire.

Spiritual Creation Exercise

Write down all the spiritual things you already believe in. Just write the first thing that comes to mind. Write free-form, do not worry about grammar or punctuation or what others think. Just take a breath, let loose, let it flow, and write. Look inside and let it speak directly to you, let your soul speak. Include all the spiritual ideas, urgings, dreams, and insights you have ever had.

Now look at what resonates within your very soul. Consider the things you miss or you want to put in place that are important to you. Is there a pattern or a path that speaks to you? Think about what you want to learn more about. If there is an item or pattern emerging, then that is the beginning of finding your true spiritual path as you continue to explore this list.

Exploring your spiritual thoughts will help you get in touch with your inner self and keep you connected to what is known as your true will. True will is finding your place in the universal flow by learning who you are now, expressing yourself, and then creating the self you really want to be. Every one of us has these abilities but we must fine-tune them. We must trust our intuition. Self-trust builds a solid foundation for working the law of attraction, manifesting, and the other psychic skills.

I have seen many people choose a spiritual path and then change themselves or their lives to match that path. Most of those people did not end up having a good experience. This has led me to believe it is far better for a person to learn who they really are and what they really believe, then choose a spiritual path that most closely resembles those beliefs. This leads them to genuinely having a satisfying spiritual experience.

I know it is difficult to slug through such work, but it pays off in the long run. I hated being told I needed to do more work or study. *Nonsense,* I thought, *I am already doing what I need* and I was, but not with any consistency. Nor was I getting the end results I really wanted. I had no idea how powerful and effective I could be. The difference between my Magic then and my Magic now is stark by comparison.

MAGIC

As we investigate Magic, we begin a move into the intermediate psychic skills. Magic has many components, styles, and methods, so for the sake of brevity, I will offer the basic techniques that are present in many forms.

I once had a teacher tell me that Magic is what you say, think, and do. That is extremely simplified, yet accurate. Spells are where we see this play out. We think of what we want and we draw up the energy and focus (a "do" part). We speak our intention or desire and then we "send" it with a magical act using our will, the other "do" part. Spells, of course, are only one small part of Magic. There are the mysteries, the cosmos, the elements, and so much more.

THE LAW OF ATTRACTION

We can begin understanding Magic by learning the real law of attraction and manifestation. Here is the equation: We do an act of Magic, which activates the law of attraction. The Magic keeps the law of attraction active until it manifests our desire.

Given social media, most think that manifesting and the law of attraction means think pretty thoughts and it will happen. Not so. Like all things Magic and spiritual, it takes time, skill, and practice.

In Witchcraft, we talk about knowing the forces you are working with. In psychism and Magic, you are the force you are working with.

When you teach yourself something new, it is helpful to know how you learn. Knowing this and using it as a tool makes for greater success and makes the law of attraction work better for you because the law of attraction and manifesting operate on clarity.

So ask yourself if you can meditate regularly with success, if you can focus well. Think about whether you are an impulsive person or restless and how you manage that. Are you someone who does not put much effort into things? Consider if you know the difference between what you want and what is actually the right thing for you, because there is a big difference between the two! Reflect on whether you truly, with all your being, believe that thoughts are things that can affect the universe and whether you have a poverty complex that will stand in your way. All of this work needs to go in your journal so you have it to reflect on anytime you need it.

All of the things you learn about yourself and about manifesting are the things behind the curtain of manifesting and the law of attraction not said to you by most who write about it. They are also the things that make the law of attraction more successful once they are known and used properly.

Following is a scientific explanation of the law of attraction.

An electromagnetic *sensitivity field* surrounds each atom. Atoms are either compatible with each other or disturbed by those electromagnetic *sensitivity fields*. When atoms that are compatible stimulate each other, they begin to *collect together* until matter that we can perceive is formed, meaning the atoms continue to collect together until they become things such as an experience or a physical item. The law of attraction is further described in June Bletzer's *The Donning International Encyclopedic Psychic Dictionary* as a result of the nature of atoms that *emanate from mental activity*.

Let me break down those descriptions. "Sensitivity field" means the energy fields all around us. Other atoms' "sensitivity field" means other energies of the things we desire. Atoms of compatibility "collect together" means like attracts like. Atoms that "emanate from mental activity" means the energy the atoms of our thoughts create and then put forth into the larger energy field of the universe.

The law of attraction is one of many universal laws. Magic and spirituality work because of the laws of nature and the laws of the universe. Each of those laws is a force of nature. One of the precepts of Witchcraft is working with the forces of nature, which means all of them, not just a few. It may be a good idea to look at what you consider to be a force of nature or a law of nature or, even better, look them up.

THE POWER OF THOUGHT

The scientific description of the law of attraction explains how thoughts are a force and can bring results. What you think becomes what you believe. What you believe becomes what you say, what you say becomes what you do.

Why is that important in spirituality and Magic? Well, if you say words you do not believe, then they have no power or impact to become physical or an action. Meaning any ritual, spell, or other Magic you do will not work.

This only reinforces to some the idea that Magic does not work. It is important to realize that Magic, spirituality, and manifesting are not something one uses like a no-fail pie crust recipe you have no connection to.

No, they are something that must come from deep within, powered by your belief and emotional connection. You must have an emotional connection to what you are doing. When that connection is coupled with your relationship to the forces of nature and the universe, you get even better results.

To work the manifesting skill using thought, you need to be very clear on the distinction between what you think you want and what is truly right for you. You also need to believe with great conviction that the universe has already provided what you have requested because the universe is infinite and provides for all.

Yes, faith and belief! You may feel you want more friends for example, and decide to manifest that in your life, then end up with friends you would rather not have. This is because you were not clear to the universe about what you wanted or what was actually right for you.

My journey is an example of that. My life was a mess and all I knew at that point was that I wanted it to be different so that is what I asked for. I ended up alone in a new place with no friends. Why? Because I was not specific. So the universe replied in its own way to my request. It filled the vacuum I left behind.

My next request was for friends. Again, I was not specific, and I ended up with people around me but they were more trouble than they were worth. The universe replied in its own way because that is how the universe works. But once I asked for friends of a like mind, however, my life changed for the better.

You may be wondering how one asks things of the universe. Well, as in all things we all have our own way, and while no one answer works for everyone, there are some consistencies to it. As stated above, first you must be clear and earnest in your request, and fully believe the universe has provided. You also need to put in some effort.

Nothing truly just falls into your lap out of thin air. You must be open to receive your desire however it comes, because it may not look like what you expect. For example, after I was ordained a Pagan Minister, the thought of hiving off into my own group kept creeping into my thoughts. Sometimes I would dismiss it, sometimes not. Sometimes I would dream about it or talk to the hubby about it. The thought just kept popping up from the back of my mind.

About six months into my ambivalence, my ex called me saying he had the perfect book for me. He was back east and had found it in a thrift store. I was stunned when it arrived because it was a book about starting your own group. The universe had replied, the book was a sign of what I was to do.

Manifestation and the law of attraction work the same way with money or anything else. You put the thought and desire out to the universe, believe it has been provided, then do your part to make it happen. How do we know it is what the universe provided? If it is the right thing, it will come fairly easy. Doors will open, or an item suddenly will be on sale way below cost but you have to be looking at the ads or stores to see it. You must be patient and keep it in the back of your mind and remain open to it coming in an unexpected way. Remaining open to the unexpected allows you to see the signs of the universe and synchronicity.

For example, my husband wanted a futon. Normally they are $400 or more, which is not in our budget. I put that desire out to the universe. When I could, I looked in the usual places for one in our price range, but not obsessively so. Manifesting is like holding a wet bar of soap. You hold it gently, loosely. If you hold it tightly, it will slip out of your hand.

About a month later, I had a ton of things to do in town. It was a day of one thing right after the other. A futon was the furthest thing from my mind that day. Yet in the middle of it when I really did not have time, my intuition nagged at me to go to a thrift store.

I even argued with my intuition saying I did not have time! Yet it persisted, so I went. As I walked in the door, there was the perfect futon for only fifty bucks! Not only was the futon there, but a friend of mine was also available to help me move it. It all just came together! It is in this way the universe provides what we want to manifest.

What is happening when we near the object of our desire? The like atoms we have been sending out are resonating, and vibrating energy with the atoms of the object we desire, which is then felt by our intuition. If we do not pay attention to it, we can miss what the universe has sent us. It is the forces of nature at work not only within us but all around us.

Working with manifesting, and the real law of attraction combined with synchronicity brings results not only in creating your life or bringing material goods to you, but it greatly increases your intuition and psychic skills, which will assist you in creating your life.

Chapter 4
STEPPING ASIDE

The stepping-aside practice is essential to psychic skills. However, there a few more steps to learn before we get there. Learning to let go in life and in spirituality is the precursor to stepping aside.

Mastery of all the previous skills is needed to practice psychic letting go and stepping aside. You will combine these skills into one effort that will result in you shifting your consciousness into an altered state for another task as you prepare for more advanced psychic skills.

LETTING GO IN PSYCHISM

Letting go in psychism differs from letting go in daily life. In psychic letting go, you release your daily consciousness briefly to apply your psychic consciousness to another task. When you use your intuition or listen to your inner self, you let go on a psychic level. You do this by shifting your consciousness to an altered state. This type of letting go is used in ritual, meditation, spellwork, channeling, divination, and trance. Stepping aside is needed in dreamwork, trance, and astral travel.

There are paradoxes in letting go. For example, when you give up control, you find control. In letting go of the search for the center, you become centered. Some of us are better at it than others. Knowing how to let go in our everyday life helps maintain our foundation; letting go psychically allows information to be sent and received. This kind of letting go is a dance between fear and trust on another level because we are dealing with the unknown and the beyond. Keep in mind, these are tools to use when you can, not something you are expected to achieve and sustain to be enlightened. We must always remember we are human and fallible.

By working on the following skills, you prepare for crossing the threshold and learn to work in liminal space. Liminal space is the space between one space and the next. The liminal spaces psychics work in are the space between one world and the next and beyond even that.

Fear

Any fear or doubt can block the whole process. Some people fear the unknown. Some fear they will not be safe, or they will look ridiculous to others. Some people fear they will not know what to do or are afraid of what may come. Some fear not being in control. Some people are even afraid of silence and space. There are many valid fears and sometimes folks have fears of which they are not even aware. This work will show you those fears.

Moving past them is beneficial in many ways; however, it takes learning what that fear feels like to allow you to mentally step past it. In psychism, we must be able to step beyond our comfort zone and into new experiences. Dealing with trust and fear at this level takes faith and is a fearsome dance between the two.

Faith

Faith is a word for which we all have a different definition. Faith has been defined as an absolute belief and absolute trust. Faith is not having no fear, but rather acting even though you have fear. It is a complete belief in the unseen but somehow known.

With faith, you believe that what you need is going to be there even while taking a risk. This is called stepping out on faith. It requires one to let go completely and trust that no matter what happens the outcome will be what is meant to be.

The best example of stepping out on faith I have ever experienced was some years ago when my family and I were driving up to Mt. Ashland. We were on our way to go sledding and skiing. The road was narrow and curvy. One side was straight uphill, the other side was straight downhill. The only resistance to going over the edge on the downhill side was a three-foot-thick snowbank. On the way up, I hit a patch of ice and the car began to spin.

At first, I was scared. I tried everything to steer and stop the car. Then I heard a voice within say, "Let go of the wheel." In that moment, I knew there was nothing more I could do. I was stepping out on faith. A calm came over me. I closed my eyes and let go of the wheel.

The car continued to spin at twenty miles an hour for what felt like forever as time seemed to slow down. In my sudden calm, I sat there with my hands up and my eyes closed while my family screamed at me to do something. When the car came to a stop it was surreal. I opened my eyes to see what had happened. The front of the car was two feet deep into the three-foot snowbank on the downhill side. The front wheels were barely touching the ground, about to go off the edge.

My family was shaken, and people came to help and make sure we were okay. Surprisingly, I was smiling, extremely grateful, and trembling. I had stepped out on faith knowing that other forces were in play. The people who stopped were able to push our car back onto the road. The car was not damaged, and we were able to go on our way.

That story is a drastic example of stepping out on faith, letting go, and completely stepping aside. I had to put aside everything I had been taught, all my instincts and reactions, and even my thought process. I had to put it all on pause, let go, and step aside to survive. In psychism, Magic, and the beyond, our lives are not at stake, but our mental capacity could be. These skills are our protection.

Caution

The act of stepping aside is one of consciously shifting your consciousness to an altered state. This can be a difficult thing for one's psyche. This work is deeper than the work done in previous chapters and may bring up issues and emotions you will not expect. The work may push you beyond your comfort zone and bring up fears and doubts, all of which need to be addressed while completing the following exercises. This is where we roll up our sleeves and do the gritty work of psychism and Magic. Please make sure you have a support system you can rely on in place before doing this work. Before you begin doing the work, I recommend reading through the next section and the exercises and journaling on how the thought of doing this work makes you feel and think.

Stepping aside is a more intense dance between faith, trust, and fear than letting go. It is a conscious act of pushing your ego, fear, and entire personality aside to let the psychic process happen. In my example above, it can take you to the edge and ask you to step off. There is much in psychism that requires you to step outside your comfort zone and continue onward; some call it threshold or precipice work, which is working on the very edge of things. In psychism, Magic, and Witchcraft we often work outside our comfort zone. This work get us ready for that.

The act of stepping aside is the moment when everything in the universe is suspended leaving only total consciousness as you move into a liminal space between two different levels of consciousness. You remove yourself from the equation and let the other side take over.

THE PRACTICE OF STEPPING ASIDE

There are various levels of stepping aside and some levels include the pause and scan skills. However, the real work comes when we deeply let go of it all. You can experience moments similar to stepping aside in meditation, or astral work. However, the goal here is to go deeper than ever before and practice the skills consciously with great focus. Please read all parts of the exercise before you begin. If you have any feelings or if any fears come up, journaling is recommended to address them before completing the work.

The following exercise is a five-part complex meditation that should be guided. I recommend finding a friend whose voice you like; let them record the exercises for you and sit with you while you work through the steps. You can record it yourself and work them alone if you feel confident enough. Give enough pause at each place where there is an action required.

I recommend taking time to process between each part. Practice each part so you can do it without your mind jumping to other, more comfortable things. This work takes disciplined practice and effort and it is important to master each part before moving to the next one. Be patient and gentle with yourself as you work through each exercise and be sure to do self-care after each part.

Stepping Aside Exercise, Part 1

Begin with the pause meditation. When you reach the puddle at your feet with your mind calm and aware, dive into the puddle. Feel the water on your skin as your inner self passes through the puddle. See or feel it clearly in your mind in every detail and relish in the sensation of it.

As you arrive, it is dark; breathe and relax. Let yourself adjust to the dark. Feel it, listen to it. Observe how it feels to your body and your mind. Let the dark become a safe and comfortable place. Breathe and remain calm and focused in the dark for at least five minutes, safe and confident. When you become comfortable and stable there, begin the process of bringing yourself back.

Practice this until you master it before moving on to part 2.

Stepping Aside Exercise, Part 2

The second part of the exercise builds the skill of getting to know the inner you and what that inner you feels like to your mind and senses. The goal is to be familiar with what you feel like to your own mind when it pushes against your consciousness.

You will need to combine the pause meditation and the stepping aside exercise, part 1, and practice them until you are once again focused and comfortable in the darkness. While in the darkness, breathe and ground yourself just like you would if awake. Then stand in the darkness, calm and relaxed, focusing on your breathing. Now in the darkness, you begin to see a shape appear. That shape is you.

Breathe steadily and keep your focus. Stay at least ten feet away from yourself and do not speak to yourself or let the self speak to you. Remain calm and notice all the details of what you look like. What are you wearing? What does your face look like? Observe what it feels like in your mind and body to see yourself.

If your breathing has quickened, slow it down. Take a few moments to observe, sense, relax, and breathe.

Before you move on to part 3, practice this part until you are perfectly comfortable seeing yourself.

Stepping Aside Exercise, Part 3

To do this part of the exercise, again combine the previous steps. Once you are ten feet from yourself, step closer; stand about three feet away from your inner self. Pause and notice what it feels like to approach yourself. Is there a quickness in your chest? Open your senses and fully feel your inner self. Breathe, calm any intensity, and stay gently focused and on task. Do not let your being uncomfortable stop you from completing this part of the exercise. If there is angst, breathe through it, remain calm, and continue.

The inner self is only there to let you know how its presence feels in your mind, emotions, and body. What does this inner self feel like to your mind and all your senses? Get to know the feel of your inner self well. Allow your mind to share this space and time with yourself for at least five minutes and then for as long as you are able. When you are ready, leave the meditation.

When you are done with this part, I urge self-care. Do not stand up right away. Breathe, readjust your vision and your senses. Just sit for a moment. Then get something to drink and eat; chocolate works wonders. Then ground your energy back to the earth. You can do that just by going outside and looking around. Please do self-care after each part of this work, which includes journaling or talking to someone.

Practice this part until being near yourself in the dark is no longer intense. This work is designed so you can recognize that part of you when it presents itself no matter what you are doing or where you are, both during your waking or sleeping life. Knowing this self allows you to keep it from interfering during other practices such as divination, ritual, trance, and many others.

You will have mastered this part of the exercise when you know the inner self by the feel of it, both mentally and emotionally, no matter when or how it presents.

While doing any part of this exercise you may feel a tingling rush through your body as you meet yourself. You may have a sense of falling as you go into the darkness. These sensations are the results of several things happening at once. Your vibrations are rising, and there is a physical release from your body occurring at the same time. That is all normal. That is your response to crossing the threshold. The body is going on autopilot, a state where it knows what to do with no interference, no restrictions, and no beliefs holding it back so just breathe through it and let it happen. Your body and mind are becoming aware of the shift in consciousness. When you feel this, do not let it stop you; rather, just recognize it for what it is and move on. Some people report this part of the exercise feeling like a combination of meditation, astral lifting, and lucid dreaming.

It reminds me of learning to float in the water. You must relax everything, not think too much, and tilt back to let your body do what comes naturally and float. Do not fear being unable to come back, as some do. That cannot happen because our consciousness is at work.

There is an awareness of the energy and vibrations that linger in our consciousness. These energies and vibrations keep you on the edge of conscious control. With them in place, it is easy to come back at will once the event is over.

Please address any issues this part of the exercise brings up for you. Name those intense feelings. Reflect on how it felt to meet yourself. The processing after the exercise allows you to fully get to know that inner self, which is the main goal.

Stepping Aside Exercise, Part 4

To begin, again combine all previous parts of the stepping aside exercise until you have mastered them.

Once in the darkness, get ten feet from your inner self. Calm any intensity and walk toward yourself; allow yourself to feel your inner presence as you get close. Breathe, and calmly and confidently walk past your inner self and on into the deeper darkness of the mind.

This darkness has a different feel; it is quieter, thicker, heavier, calm, and peaceful. Breathe, relax, and get familiar with this place. You will have mastered this part when you are comfortable enough to just be in the darkness and do nothing.

Stepping Aside Exercise, Part 5

As you have done previously, combine all parts of the exercise to mastery before completing this part.

Once in the second and deeper darkness, begin using your scanning and sensing as you gently breathe. Now open yourself, pause, and listen; continue to breathe gently.

Calmly and gently let this space know that you are there to listen. Gently focus on your breathing and stay relaxed while you wait. This is the place where your everyday consciousness meets your subconscious. You are now in your subconscious mind and lucid. Spend as much time here as you can. Keep sensing and listening and let the experience happen.

When you are ready, leave the exercise slowly and make sure to do your self-care when you are done. You have now successfully and consciously shifted your consciousness into an altered state.

Journal all your experiences, talk to others about them, and ask yourself what it was like and what you noticed, felt, and learned.

The first few times you do this exercise, you may only get darkness. Other times you may get visuals, colors, shapes, or people, perceive other information, or get some other kind of stimuli.

You will have mastered stepping aside when you can complete all the parts of the exercises in one sitting at will and comfortably.

Sometimes you may feel a nudge from your intuition pulling you into an altered state. This occurs when you are familiar with the various vibrational shifts around you. When that happens, there is always a reason. It is usually something you should know or information about someone close to you. Once you have mastered stepping aside, working the more common psychic skills will be much easier.

COMMON PSYCHIC SKILLS

In the rest of this chapter, we will look at the more common psychic skills. To practice these skills, you will need mastery of the exercises in this and previous chapters.

All of the following skills will begin with the skills you have learned to combine previously, so keep your notes close.

EMPATHIC SKILLS

Chapters 1 through 3 are like a handbook for someone with empathic skills. Those chapters work well for extra sensitive people, those on an autistic threshold, ADD folks, borderline personality disorder folks, and those who are bipolar as well. There is no Magic pill that solves it all, but the skills you have learned here so far sure make it easier to manage that extra sensitive part of us, no matter what label it has.

An empath has been defined as one who psychically tunes in to the emotional state of another person, an animal, a group, or things. They sense what others feel and they feel it intensely, sometimes with their whole body. What an empath feels can at times be so intense it is difficult for them to know which feelings are theirs and which belong to someone else.

Clairempathic

A clairempathic is defined as a psychic who receives visual information along with the senses within their mind that are the attitudes, feelings, or emotions of another.

Having an empathic skill can be overwhelming to some people. Some empaths describe it as feeling everything, from everyone all at once. This is because empathic skills have a wide range. They can go from *I know you're lying*, to overemotional crying jags because they feel something so much.

Anxiety, overthinking, doubt, and insecurity are often the companions of an empath. It is vital for an empath to know what belongs to them and what does not. When you recognize what does not belong to you, it allows you to put it in its proper place in your life. Which means you no longer have to feel it. More skills for empaths are listed in chapter 11.

The one thing that gave me the most freedom from the impact of empathic intensity was discovering that I can choose what to do with what I feel. The realization that I do not have to just let feelings happen and overwhelm me freed me. (The first three chapters are the summation of my learning that lesson.)

Many empaths are driven almost compulsively to help others with their issues. This occurs because of how strongly an empath feels and because we as humans are socially conditioned to ease the suffering of others.

Often, however, people confuse compassion with rescuing rather than helping. When this happens, it only further complicates and confuses what the empath is receiving.

Compassion is feeling and caring for another person or animal while acknowledging that how they feel is not their responsibility to take on. Empathy is the ability to not only understand another's feelings but also put yourself in their shoes to the point that you feel what they are going through in that situation. This still does not mean that what the other person is experiencing is your responsibility. Having empathy means you feel deeply or relate to what they are experiencing as you experience their moment with them. But you must give them space to have their own experience.

Rescuing versus Helping

Recognizing the difference between rescuing and helping is one of the most common problems empaths have. Knowing the difference gives an empath clarity and freedom from emotion.

Rescuing is intervening in another person's life—intervening to the point where you are not letting them live the full effects of their own emotions or the consequences of their choices. Many people think they are helping when in fact they are rescuing, enabling, and becoming codependent. I know this is a harsh thing to look at but defining and dealing with this is an emapth's greatest asset.

With rescuing, the person wanting to be rescued must have another person present to safely feel anything. After a while, being with someone like this makes you feel consumed and exhausted, and can lead you to resent them. This kind of relationship ends up with the dependent person being labeled an energy vampire. The term *energy vampire* means that every time you are with a particular person you come away feeling drained. If you find this is true of someone you are dealing with, you are likely in the cycle of rescuing instead of helping. Rescuing is a slippery slope to be sure. The lesson on letting go and about being compassionate but not doing things for someone will assist in breaking free from this kind of relationship.

Helping

Helping, on the other hand, is allowing others to figure things out for themselves while being supportive and demonstrating compassion and empathy. Helping often includes just holding space for a friend while they go through things. Holding space is just being there. Sometimes helping is not saying or doing anything except listening. Even hugging a person when they are upset is a way of relieving you and the person from fully feeling what they need to, so you have to make a judgment call in those moments to hug or not and ask yourself why you want to hug them. We have been taught that hugging is what you do to comfort a person; in helping, you wait to hug until after the person has fully expressed and then ask permission to hug. Also in helping, you ask if they want your assistance or advice.

I know this sounds counterintuitive, but it is important for empaths and psychics to know the difference between rescuing and helping. If they don't know the difference, it can take over their lives, which can lead to a lot of emotional distress and confusion about what is real and what is not. You may think you are in the service of others, which you think is a noble cause and what you are supposed to do. But rescuing is not noble or in service of others; rescuing only serves to derail you from your own life and needs. Walking the fine line between compassion, helping, and rescuing is not easy. It takes a lot of self-evaluation and healthy boundaries. It also takes saying no, as difficult as that can be at times.

In summation, the best advice I can give an empath is this: feel the feelings of others, but do not become or live the emotion; witness it, allow it, love it and yourself, recognize it as not yours, then release it. More skills for releasing others' emotions will be discussed in chapter 10.

PATHWORKING

Pathworking is a pre-trance type of guided meditation. Others feel it is just a lighter form of trance. Either way, your brain waves are shifting to an altered state. In pathworking, the altered state is not as deep as it is in a full trance. In pathworking, you are going to a specific place for a specific reason as you would in a guided meditation. You can visit the Akashic records, the Goddess Isis, or any spirit or deity and talk to them directly. Once you go to a specific place, you have established a path and can go back anytime you like.

Pathworking is done while you are awake, as in meditation. Pathworking helps you develop a relationship with Gods, spirits, and other realms. You also can use pathworking to get to know about your past lives.

The visualization required to do stepping aside and pathworking aids in lucid dreaming, trance work, Magic, and ritual work. It stimulates the synapses in the brain. Each time you use those synapses, it trains your brain to make those connections. Eventually, you will be able to achieve the use of those synapses and shift your consciousness at will without using meditation or visualization to get there.

Literally any place, any time, any being you can think of, you can create a pathworking too. It is good to know about where you want to go, who you want to see, and where they reside before a pathworking. Doing research ahead of time also aids in your ability to respond with knowledge and respect during a pathworking. So it is wise to read up on them first.

Visualization, awareness, imagination, and stepping aside are all needed skills here. It is best to begin with something simple such as a deceased relative, or a very well-known deceased spiritual leader such as Gandhi, Buddha, or the Oracle at Delphi (see the bibliography for helpful books to read about Gandhi and the Oracle at Delphi).

You will need to set aside some time and create a quiet space where you will not be interrupted. This includes kids, phones, pets, or roommates.

For a meaningful and deep encounter, it is important to pause and give yourself time to truly see and feel each action and change in the scene. If a friend is reading the following meditation, or if you have recorded it and are playing it back, be sure to give yourself time in between each action or change of scene.

In the following pathworking meditation, you will visit the Empress from the tarot (I use the Rider-Waite Empress card for the description, but you can use any deck for this mediation). The goal is to so completely be there that you are living the moment and interacting in her realm.

Pathworking Meditation

Set your space and get comfortable. Let all the world's worries flow through your body and into the ground. Breathe to release the daily world. Get out the Empress card from a deck of tarot and look closely at the details. Note the color of the sky, the details of her dress, and so on. Once you have the details firmly in mind, put down the card.

Begin the relaxation exercise that comes before the pause meditation exercise. Dive into the pool at your feet and go to the first level of darkness. Once you are there, relax.

Now look down at your feet on the dark floor; you begin to see a golden light spreading out from under your feet. As you watch it becomes a field of wheat swaying in a gentle breeze on a sunny day. Hear the wheat rustling in the breeze and feel the plants against you as you walk through the field.

Look around and let the scene become every detail of what you saw on the tarot card. Stay with that image until you feel you are *really* there.

You are now in the realm of the Empress. Breathe in the fresh air. Let it fill your lungs and feel the sun on your skin.

As you look around, you see a rise in the center of the field with trees around the edge of the meadow you are standing in. As you look at the rise, you see a woman sitting on a red-cushioned seat. She has golden hair and flowing robes. It is the Empress of the tarot; visualize her fully in every detail, and walk toward her.

As you approach, she invites you to sit at her feet. Once you are seated, ask her what message she has for you. Do not be shy about asking questions of her, or of taking a gift from her or giving her a gift. Relax and let the vision happen. Take your time. The vision will signal you when it is time to go.

Returning from a pathworking is the same as coming back from the pause meditation. The first time you go to a place or person, that pathworking is typically guided and has a specific goal or a question to be answered. Now that the path is established in your mind, you can have a chat or experience there anytime you wish. If you have had a dream or have astral traveled and you want to go back, you can do so with pathworking.

3/12/09

I set up my space and entered the pathworking. I arrive in the darkness and as I stood looking around, the ground became sand then it becomes a vast desert. It is twilight, I see oases here and there when I notice a large structure on a hill and began walking toward it. I felt the warm sand on my feet and smelled the hot sand as the vapors rose from it. As I stood before the building, I see it is ancient and well cared for.

At the entrance, there is a stone landing in front of a huge door with pillars and statues of Anubis. As I take in the scene, one of the statues of Anubis steps forward with a spear in hand. He looks at the door; it opens as he motions for me to follow him. Inside there is a vast courtyard with hanging gardens with fountains and servants caring for them. Anubis directs me to a narrow hall to my right. As I follow him, the hall turns first one direction then the other. When it seems as if it will go on forever, I begin to get nervous about where he is taking me.

We finally come to a door; he stands next to it as it opens for me to enter. There are more gardens, an Egyptian bath, and glorious foods on a table. To my right, I see a dark-haired woman on a pile of pillows. She is being attended to by servants. I notice Anubis motioning me toward her. I get a few feet from her when she stands and unfolds wings of gold and emeralds and proclaims, "Behold! You stand before the mighty Isis, pay your respects!" Startled, I bow and stay bowed unsure of what I should do next. She comes forward and touches my arm. I look up at her. She kindly asks me to join her on the pillows where she offers me dates and we sit and talk. It was a lovely and informative visit.

Now that I have been to see Isis, I can go back anytime. Pathworking is a very useful tool when working with deities.

REMOTE VIEWING

Remote viewing is typically described as a psychic projecting their clairvoyant vision to another location to view it in detail. Clairvoyant remote viewing is worked like pathworking. You sit in a meditative state and focus on the target. Some remote viewers can employ automatic writing or drawing while using this skill.

When I do remote viewing, I get an address, the target. Then in a meditative state using clairvoyance, I can view it. I have had some very interesting remote viewing experiences as demonstrated below.

11/1/08

At 7:45 a.m. my time, I read a message from Dee, a woman from my online group. She wanted to discuss precognitive dreaming and a vibration she had in her body. As I read, I began to feel a warm calm rising from within. I connected psychically and sent my reply. I first tell her to go see a Dr. as her right ribs might need to be paid attention to. I closed my eyes and go to her remotely to do a body reading. I type as I view her. "You are afraid to open up around family. You internalize, all that fear and stress." I then see a trapped orb within her. It is a child. I can see him clearly and feel how loved he feels there within her. I then hear him as he cries "Mommy listen please!" I can see him clinging to her, his emotions are intense which startles me. I take a breath to steady myself and look again. I see a heavy-set woman with short curly hair. She lives in a trailer house with a large yard. It is a cloudy day where she is. I text all this to her then I tell her I must break off as I am feeling overwhelmed and weak and I include my phone number.

Then later that same morning…

11/1/08

9:15 a.m. my time the phone rings. I hear a woman with a Southern accent and a trembling voice. This is Dee she says. I wanted to call you and let you know you were so accurate it took my breath away! You described me perfectly. The pain on my right side is an existing gallbladder issue, how did you know that? What you said about the child is astounding! My son is autistic, and you described him perfectly too.

We talked about the possibility of the vibration being her son trying to communicate with her. While we talk, I clairvoyantly see she gives love away rather than giving it to herself. We talk about that and Edgar Cayce only to discover she lives not far from his institute and I encourage her to go. When we end the call, I am trembling. I am stunned at my own ability, at how well I could see, how accurate it was through a computer, my mind was blown too.

Several days later…

11/5/08

9 a.m. I wake from a startling clairvoyant dream. I have seen another woman from my online group arguing with her husband. In my mind, I hear "She won't win." I see her husband is intent on harming her. Telepathically I try to send her the message to get out. I get up and message her via computer.

> *At 10:45 a.m., she calls after reading my message, and says, "OMG how did you know? How is this possible?" she stammered. We were both stunned, I was so dead-on about what happened.*

These examples show how remote viewing uses clairvoyance and how accurate the viewing can be.

OUT-OF-BODY EXPERIENCE

An out-of-body experience (OBE) can occur while awake or asleep and is also known as bilocation. If you are out of your body, you are having an out-of-body experience, no matter what plane of reality you are on. OBEs are different from astral travel because, in my experience, OBEs occur only on this plane of reality, this everyday world, whereas in astral travel you can go to any plane, world, or reality.

An out-of-body experience is not a paranormal experience. It is a psychic event experienced in an altered state of consciousness. An OBE is the subconsciousness separating from the everyday consciousness.

While accounts of OBEs vary, there are some common characteristics. Most commonly reported is the existence of a second subtle body that becomes the vehicle for travel. To some individuals, this body is usually invisible, though the person viewing can sense its presence. If seen, the body appears to be an apparition. Some individuals report having no form at all or being points of light or presence of energy.

In this energy form, OBE travelers report moving about the earth plane like apparitions, passing through walls and solid objects. They say they travel with the speed of thought. (Astral travel to nonearthly realms, called the astral planes, are much different and include being able to make contact with objects and beings who feel real and solid.) Most documented claims of OBEs report not being able to interact with places or people. The onset of OBEs can occur spontaneously during waking consciousness, and before, during, or after sleep.

They can occur during severe illness or in times of great stress. OBEs often occur during trauma and/or in a moment of intense fear. They can also be induced during hypnosis, meditation, and other techniques. The OBE is often preceded by a perception of strong and high-frequency vibrations. Some individuals report leaving through their head or solar plexus or simply rising and floating away. Reentry occurs typically in the same way as the lifting out.

TRANCE WORK

Trance can be described as an altered state in which the psychic shifts their consciousness to have an experience in the etheric world. A trance is an in-depth experience with spirits, deities, ancestors, or yourself in the etheric world. Etheric is often described as the invisible world; I call it "The Beyond" because it lies well beyond our everyday world and the basic or common psychic events.

Note: Mastering the stepping aside skill exercises is required for trance work.

Trance is a deep altered state of mind and is almost hypnotic; you will step out of this world and reality entirely until nothing else exists but your experience of your visions. In trance, the etheric world beyond leads the experience, not your consciousness as in pathworking. Your body is in such a deep state of rest that it makes the body feel like it is sleeping. When you begin trance work, you should have a general idea or goal in mind, like in meditation or pathworking, to begin your focus.

Trance Exercise

For this exercise, we will once again visit the Empress from the tarot. To reach a trance state, begin with the pause meditation and continue through the five parts of the stepping aside exercise until you are in the second level of darkness. Breathing gently, allow yourself to begin seeing shapes in the darkness and let the image of the Empress materialize. Once you see her, step aside and let the rest happen. She will lead the experience from there. She will also signal you as to when the event is over.

Coming out of trance takes a bit longer than with pathworking or meditation and you may feel groggy, so take your time and use self-care and ground yourself afterward.

Trance is transformative. It is an experience in which you can explore the deeper recesses of your mind. When applied to shadow work, trance can be very helpful.

Most of my trances take more than an hour; some have taken up to three hours. I have had some that reveal magical practices and rituals. I usually trance in front of my altar and occasionally right as I fall asleep. Which form I choose depends on my goals. Following is one of my more memorable trances from my journal.

8/15/19

I began the trance as I was falling asleep. I held the Magician card and focused on every detail. I laid it down and kept the image firm in my mind as I drifted off. As I become lucid in my dream I see the images of the card floating disjointedly. When they came together, I was in the same room as the Magician. I looked at the tools on the table and the infinity sign and considered how he had all the tools and infinite possibilities before him. I asked him to show me a day in his life.

I wanted to know what his world was like. He tells me he always keeps the tools with him. He holds up the staff and tells me it is used in ritual to call the Element of Air. It is used in that way because it was once a living organism that produced oxygen and cleaned air. He proceeds to show me how he uses the staff in ritual as he calls the Element of Air. He goes on to explain how it also opens portals to all realms of air. Next, he combines the staff with the infinity sign and opens the portal to the realms of air.

I see many realms and worlds appear before me. The Magician informs me that the realm of Air holds all worlds of the things we associate with air. Worlds and planes of intellect, psychism, breath, dawn, East, atmosphere, levitation, and invisibility. He tells me with the tools used properly in this way, we can travel to these realms.

He closes the Air portal and takes up the sword. He says it is used to call the Element of Fire. He talks about how its metal ore is formed by the fire deep in the earth then is dug up by the passion of men, who then forge it by fire into a sword. He moves to the South end of the room and with a ritual opens the portal to the realms of fire. As the Fire portal opens, I see the realms and planes of all things fire. Worlds that are all deserts. Worlds and planes that are anything volcano related. There are realms, and planes of transformation, passion, shapeshifting, creation, the spark of life, and all newly forming places before me.

He then closes the Fire portal and moves to the West. He takes up the chalice and opens the portal of water. Before me, I see all kinds of planes where water dwells. I see that water includes all dark realms, planes of laughter, tears, emotions, snow, and ice.

To the North, he opens the Earth portal with the pentacle. It leads to all places of growing things, plants, ground dwellers, caves, snow, and magnetic realms which can be traveled to through the Aurora Borealis.

When he was finished, I asked him what his part in the deck was. He said to tell you, you have all the tools you need before you to not limit their use, be creative with them because you and the tools have infinite possibilities. With that, he waved his staff and was gone through a portal, and the trance was done.

I have since changed how I use the tools on the altar. This experience shows how trance is very useful in shadow work, working with deities, and having spiritual and magical experiences in many realms. Psychometry, on the other hand, is like a mix of clairvoyance, divination, and kinetic skills

PSYCHOMETRY

In *Meta-Psychometry: Key to Power and Abundance,* Gavin and Yvonne Frost define psychometry as reading memories and energies of the past left behind in an object as it relates to the person who owned it.

In almost all writings on the subject, authors speak only of reading objects. The theory is that an object can retain the vibrations and energies of the people who owned it. The diviner then receives those vibrations and energies through touch and sees or senses them in the mind as memories coming from the object. Which further supports the concept that thoughts are things.

I can read inanimate objects moderately well. I am better at reading trees, walls, some stones, or in some instances the ground rather than the usual personal item.

However, I read people by touch very well. My best friend once said, "Do not let her hug you unless you want her to know everything about you." She said it with laughter and love, but it was a warning for the person to shield because it is true.

Without realizing it, most people broadcast their surface thoughts and emotions quite readily. It is an energy people put out when they inadvertently broadcast. I can feel and clairvoyantly see that broadcasted energy when I am within ten feet of most people. That energy alerts my psychic skills and prompts me to scan that energy more deeply. In the scan, my empathic skills tell me their mood and if it is good, mad, bad, deeply troubled, and so on.

Then, if I choose to hug the person, I open all my senses to let in what they are broadcasting inadvertently. When I hug them, my clairvoyance gives me the visuals, my empathy the feelings, and my claircognizance provides the knowing. This shows how individual skills can combine and be useful.

Psychometry Exercises

There are games that help build psychometry skills you can do with anyone. They can be fun to do at parties too.

To begin, close your eyes and relax. Now rub your hands together vigorously, especially the fingertips. This will activate the sensory pads there. With eyes still closed, begin to gently rub your clothing or whatever is next to you with your fingertips. Pay attention to everything you feel, every texture every bump, whatever it is. This exercise stimulates the sensory pads in your fingers.

Many people are surprised at all the subtle things they feel which they never would have noticed before. Thus, this exercise is excellent to build awareness training too.

Once you have gotten familiar with what your finger sensory pads can feel, try the exercise again but this time touch a paper you are not familiar with that has images and colors on it. Rub your fingers gently around the picture and use your sense of touch to focus on what it tells you.

The goal is to see if you can feel when the graphic changes or the color changes. If you get a clairvoyant image with changes do not be surprised.

For another skill builder, take four different colored pieces of construction paper and tear a small piece from each one. Put the pieces into a bag or bowl out of your sight and mix them up. Now, with eyes closed reach in and grab one. Rub the piece between your fingers to see if you can tell which color you have picked (no peeking!).

Whole-Body Psychometric Readings

The first order of business in a body reading is to inform the client this is a reading done by touch. I inform them no personal areas will be touched. I may touch the top of their head, the back of their neck, their shoulders, their entire back, and their sides, chest, or knees. Always ask their permission to do so and allow them to tell you what touch is acceptable and where and make changes as needed. Next, I use relaxed, casual conversation and we laugh together over iced tea. This builds trust and gets a person open, relaxed, and receptive.

Next, I use a relaxing, breathing, and grounding exercise to get us both focused. At this point, I shift my consciousness for the skill set I am about to use. I have my client sit on a stool without a back and I usually stand behind them as I read. I have them take one more deep breath and exhale before I touch the top of their head to begin the reading.

Body Zones

As I have mentioned, our bodies have a memory. That idea has been expressed in many ways over time. We know thoughts are things that have energy and emanate a vibration. So too are the things that occur to or in our bodies—not just injuries and illness but stresses and memories as well. Our bodies store all of that and when certain parts of the body are touched it evokes that memory again. This fact was made apparent to me during two years of medical massage after my car accident. I was often surprised at what memories or emotional release came from my various parts as I was being massaged.

These stored vibrations and energies are what I read from a person. It is much like how a masseur can find places where you are tense or in pain that you were not even aware of. Over the years, I have discovered there are zones of the body that retain different things:

Top of the Head

Current decisions. This is where the most pressing questions are stored; questions like, Should I take that job? When I touch the top of the head, I usually get a swirl of thought, then one or two thoughts that are most pressing will noticeably stand out. In this zone, the thoughts are more linear than conceptual. Sometimes, I will receive the answer before getting the question or any kind of visual. In reading a friend one day, I put my hand on the top of his head and the word *no* came loud and clear. "Whatever it is you're thinking, the answer is no," I said. He was wondering if he should do business with an individual.

I asked him to think about that person and I put my hand back on the top of his head. I was able to pick up more detail on what could go wrong through clairvoyant and empathic skills.

I find clairvoyant images to be more linear; empathic receiving is more of a conceptual feeling I get in my chest or stomach. Sometimes, I get clairvoyance first then an empathic feel. Other times, I get an empathic feel then clairvoyant images to back up what I am feeling. When you have multiple psychic skills, they will interchange at their own will so it is important to be flexible but also aware—which is another reason why knowing your skills well is important.

Neck

Personal stress. This zone extends from the base of the head down to the first four vertebrae between the shoulders. Stress includes anything that stresses you, such as personal life, coworkers, health, family, or money.

Shoulders

Personal concerns of security. This zone includes the trapezius muscles and the shoulder blades. These concerns can range from transportation issues, housing, and food to other issues of survival.

Below the Shoulders

Issues about our relationships, all of them. This zone can extend to the middle of the back.

Middle of the Back

Deeper, more personal relationship issues. In this zone, issues can be felt on into the ribcage. The relationship issues I typically find here are the surface issues with life partners, sexual partners, or those they deeply love. In this zone, I also find sleep issues, how tired they are, or their desire for rest. I can see how a person sleeps on one side or the other and why. I can tell if that is a good thing or not. I can see how that information relates to a specific relationship, their health, the bed they sleep in, or the person they sleep with.

Lower Back

Deep relationship issues. This zone is just below the ribs. Health issues, if there are any, are here too because inside the body is where the major organs are located.

Small of the Back

The things that make a person uncomfortable. This zone is from the waist to just above the beltline. These are the things they do not want to talk about but are well aware of. Things they do not want to admit, or what they struggle with the most. It can be truths about themselves or others.

Spine Below the Beltline

Hidden family-of-origin and childhood issues. Before reading this zone, I always ask permission. I let them know what I am likely to find and ask if they want that information revealed. This zone is just below the beltline and above the cleft of the bottom, the tailbone. I rarely find anything nice and sweet here. This is why I inform people how revealing and deep one of my readings can be. Reading this zone is intense work for all involved.

I have had such readings take five hours. Not in the reading itself, but in the processing of the information revealed. You need to be ready for anything you reveal here. Gentleness, compassion, and understanding are required. Not for you, but for the person you are reading.

Revealing such deeply personal information carries a responsibility. If you are going to step through a person's defenses, you need to be prepared for the emotional release that comes after. For deep readings, I make sure the space is private. Also make sure there is enough time set aside to assist the individual with processing afterward. I also provide something to drink and a snack for grounding us both. Following is the notes on one of my readings.

12/12/08

The subject is a 19 yr. old young man, once he arrives, I set the space by lighting candles and smudging. He sits on a stool in the center of the room as I guide him through a relaxation exercise. I stand in front of him and hold his hands for a moment with my eyes closed. This begins the connection and exchange of energy.

As we hold hands, I begin to receive information as I start to feel the warmth and compassion that the young man has within him. I verbally encourage him to breathe and relax. I then stand behind him and touch the top of his head and the images in my mind begin to flow like fast-moving clips of film. Images of school and home. As I touch the back of his neck, I feel static and stress. I move my hand to between his shoulder blades, and in his voice, I hear "brother not nice" and see the images of his brother and some of their conflicts. I move my hand to the middle of his back, and I mentally hear him clearly say "Always messing with me." I feel the anger from the brother toward the young man. As I do I also mentally see the brother and know he is violent and malicious.

I move my hand to the young man's lower back. I see his Mom and I feel love and shame. As I touch near his waist on his back, I hear "I can't do this" from him. I then see he is afraid of a man. I look deeper as I feel his severe stress and anxiety about this man. As I am sensing this, I suddenly feel a punch in the gut. I see more violence and encourage the young man to breathe and relax.

Due to the intensity, I ease up and put my hands on his shoulders and run my thumbs down his back to help him relax. I tell him I can see that his brother picks on him mentally, but not physically, and continue by saying you love your mom, but the sound of her voice annoys you, it is not what she says but how she sounds. He chuckles and says yes.

I now have one hand on a shoulder, the other on the middle of his back, and I see from my visons that his mom thinks he is the one that agitates his brother, who mom protects. I relate this to him, and he confirms. I touch the small of his back and get a vision of him walking down the stairs as he jumps away in fear from a picture of the man I saw before. In my vision I see the man's spirit had jumped out at him to scare him and he falls back against the wall in fear. He begins to resist so I move my hands to his shoulders, and he relaxes but continues to block me. I put my hand on his forehead, I again see the stairs. The young man is against the wall in fear as a black shape pushes him and then moves past him. "Who is the man on the stairs?" I ask him. "My dad," he says as I feel his pulse rise and his breath quicken.

I relax him again and I ask if it is okay to touch his chest and he agrees. I feel intense fear, I hear yelling and screaming and intimidation. I tell him I can feel his dad and he replies he was not a very nice man. Then I move behind him and relax him and put my hand on the back of his neck and move it down to the small of his back. There I see the image of his girl rise in my mind's eye, I mention this and he seems very happy with her and then he cuts me off. The reading is done.

I tell him it is okay to open himself to the girl, that he is not the only man to feel this way and he laughs as I offer him some tea and says, "I am glad to know that I am not the first to feel that way," as he chuckles.

I encourage him to not be so serious in school and to have some fun. Then we begin to discuss his brother messing with his head and tell him I see that the brother is more devilish than his mother knows; this relaxes him, and he smiles and nods his head.

I teach him ways to block his brother and manage his anger. We talk about his not understanding his mother's protection of his brother when his father died. We talk about his resentment towards her for that and his feelings of abandonment. Silently, he begins to cry saying how did you know that?

I comfort him and say it is ok, we will work through it. Just feel it for a moment and breathe. I wait a few moments, then I ask him about his girl, bringing him up out of the negative space. I close by telling him the best thing for him to do is to move out. "I did last week," he says looking at me in surprise. Well, that is good I say, now you can have your girl over and we laugh. I encourage him to see a therapist about the other family issues before he leaves, and he tells me he feels much better, and thanks so much.

This is only one example of the depth of such readings. It clearly demonstrates how the reader needs to be available for the client emotionally. In all of this let us not forget about ethics. In psychism, the basic rule for ethics is about timing and sensitivity when revealing what you know, as seen in the above example. It goes like this: if you are perceptive enough to know the truth, then you must also be perceptive enough to know when to reveal it, and to do so only for the best interest of the person you are revealing to.

I will only do one such reading a day because the self-care needed afterward is extensive. Depending on the reading, the self-care can take several days. I have a process of first eating and grounding then watching animals, cartoons, or travel shows of beautiful places on TV. I do this to restore and clean my inner and outer vision. It also rebalances my emotional intensity.

All of the examples given show how these skills can progress from being a simple psychic skill to an intermediate psychic skill, and grow to being an advanced skill, which is the goal as you progress. So practice and have fun with them.

Chapter 5
ADVANCING YOUR SKILLS

Advanced psychic skills are fun; however, they take practice, skill, and focus, so begin with the basic skills found at the beginning of the chapter and work your way up. With these skills, we begin to look at the different ways of thinking, mainly from linear to conceptual thinking. Linear thinking is the typical way we think every day. Conceptual thinking, on the other hand, is less well-known and is a way of thinking in loose ideas, abstract ideas, or general notions. Most psychic skills require conceptual thinking.

CLAIRVOYANCE

Clair is French for "clear" and *voyance* means "vision." Clairvoyance overlaps with many other psychic skills, such as clairaudience, clairsentience, telepathy, precognition, and empathic senses. Some folks only have one psychic skill they are good at, which is great. However, I suspect many have more than one skill. I also believe there are more clairvoyants out there than are recognized. Defining clairvoyance is important because when you know the boundaries and abilities of each skill, it provides better control and clarity.

Clairvoyance is a general ability among humans. Ever wonder how parents know what kids are doing? Usually, it is intuition; they get a sudden nudge that makes them look up and say, "Wait, what is going on?" Then they scan and can usually tell. If a parent has clairvoyance, they will see what is going on.

Clairvoyance has been acknowledged, used, and cultivated since ancient times. Prophets, fortune-tellers, shamans, wizards, witches, cunning folk, and seers through all ages have employed clairvoyance. Like other skills, clairvoyance can be used on an intermediate or advanced level. In its highest form, clairvoyance is the viewing of nonphysical planes, the astral, the etheric, the spiritual worlds, and the beings that inhabit them. This includes the auric field surrounding all things in nature.

A clairvoyant is a psychic who can tune in to others and the etheric world, and see things through images in their mind. A clairvoyant can interpret those images based on their own symbolism. Visual input can be conceptual or linear in nature. This means a clairvoyant can perceive current objects, events, or people who cannot be known through the normal senses.

Clairvoyance Exercises

Find a friend or family member and ask them to find a picture but not show it to you. Have them focus on the picture for a while and then put it in an envelope. Now sit face-to-face or back-to-back and have them keep the image in their mind.

Use the pause meditation to relax and clear your mind and let the images come. You may get several images or thoughts at first. Stay with it until one clear image comes to mind. When you are done, tell them what you saw and ask them to reveal the contents of the envelope. This can be fun at parties too.

For another exercise, when you first wake up see if you can tune in to someone you are close to. Look to see if you can tell what they are doing, what they are wearing, or how they are feeling. Note the time of day and then contact them to see how accurate you were.

Another fun exercise is to tune in to someone you are speaking to on the phone to see if you can tell what they are wearing or where they are.

Traveling Clairvoyance

Traveling clairvoyance is the ability to cast your inner vision and awareness across a room or distance to see what is happening somewhere else; this is similar to remote viewing. When using traveling clairvoyance, I shift my consciousness from the present moment to the item or person I wish to tune in to. Then I use pause and scan to cast my inner vision and awareness toward my goal. I can generally tell what is going on anywhere I choose.

Once, when deeply engaged in a conversation with a friend, I got a clear vision of a man sitting on the curb outside; he was someone my friend knew. With my inner vision/clairvoyance, I could see him hanging his head in his hands. My empathy revealed he was sad, confused, and needed someone to talk to. I excused myself and went to talk to him. He was grateful and I was able to help him.

It has been a challenge for some of my partners to live with my clairvoyance. One time, I was in the house doing artwork while my husband was out in the garage. He had been out there most of the day when I suddenly had a strong vision and I empathically could feel what he was thinking and feeling. He was having uncomfortable thoughts about himself and his dad, so I went to comfort him. It surprised him and he felt I had invaded his private thoughts, which I had. I felt terrible when I realized what I had done.

This raises a point on the etiquette and ethics of psychism. Someone once told me, "Just because you know the truth does not mean you have to say it." People deserve their privacy and to sort out their own issues. With our skills and gentle guidance, we can ethically lead folks to resolution without disclosing what we already know.

Medical Clairvoyance

Medical clairvoyance is the ability to see disease or illness in the human body by reading the aura, seeing the body as transparent, or touch. Edgar Cayce was one of the most famous of all medical clairvoyants of our time. Many of his books are still available, and there are still institutes in Virginia where his work continues. During his readings, he would view the Akashic records on the astral to obtain information. All of Cayce's work included remedies, cures, and much more using spatial clairvoyance. Please note that medical clairvoyance is not a replacement for clinical medical care.

Spatial Clairvoyance

Spatial clairvoyance is clairvoyant vision through distance and time beyond an individual's line of physical sight. It can be willed or unwilled and occur while awake or asleep. Spatial clairvoyance differs from remote viewing and traveling clairvoyance because in spatial clairvoyance, you can see visions of the past, into a body, into the atmosphere, to other planets and universes, and into the beyond. If you have clairvoyance, you can practice spatial clairvoyance through trance.

I break up spatial clairvoyance into two categories: distance and time.

Distance-Spatial Clairvoyance Exercise, Part 1

Prepare for trance using the pause meditation and the stepping aside exercise. Visualize yourself above Earth. See it in every detail. Visualize seeing all the people. Then visualize an energy stream going from each person and into the ground connecting them to the earth.

This visualization reminds me of the *X-Men* movie where Xavier sees all the mutants when he is in the chamber. I recommend doing this exercise often because it reminds us that we are all connected. This exercise allows an advanced psychic to check in with the pulse of the world. Eventually, this exercise will lead to being able to interact with the beings in the cosmos. Both are helpful in Witchcraft and Magic.

Distance-Spatial Clairvoyance Exercise, Part 2

Once you master part 1, go outside, stand with your eyes closed, and extend your clairvoyance into the atmosphere. Connect with it until you feel like you are breathing with it and can see the connection of all life at will. I use distance-spatial clairvoyance in ritual to call the elements and deities. I also use it in trance to visit the fates and the guardians of the watchtowers. The guardians of the watchtower are the spirits that reside in each location of each of the elements. For example, there is a guardian of the watchtower in the East where the Element of Air resides, and this is so for the other directions too.

Time-Spatial Clairvoyance Exercise

Time-spatial clairvoyance is looking into the past. For this exercise, pick a past event or person you want to see, then prepare for trance with that in mind. See it in every detail. Let the vision unfold as you drop deeper into a trance.

Another way to practice this exercise is with a friend. Ask them to think about an event you do not know about. They need to choose something they can clearly see in their mind and hold focus on. Gently yet loosely focus on what you might be receiving and keep with it for a few minutes as you relax. As you slowly come out of the trance, discuss what you experienced with your friend. Practice as often as you can. I do not recommend trying this with a friend more than twice in one day.

Time-spatial clairvoyance is an interesting skill. Once at a party, a friend of mine began sharing a past event with me that he had not told anyone about. As soon as he began to think of it, I saw it clearly in my mind. I then described it for him in full detail. He was shocked that I could so accurately describe something he had kept secret for so long. I was in my early twenties when this occurred. I had not developed any ethical filters yet; I was still in the "If I see it, I say it" mode.

CLAIRCOGNIZANCE

Claircognizance is knowing without any evidence. Claircognizants "know" specific things through their psychic perceptions that are directly manifested as thoughts. Claircognizance includes perceptions and insights regarding people, circumstances, and events in the present or future. Claircognizance does not have any visual or empathic components.

While closely related to telepathy, claircognizance is different. With telepathy, the information you receive comes from another person's thoughts. Claircognizance is a precise knowing—one you know is from your own mind. Psychics who have claircognizance are absolutely convinced of its accuracy. They just clearly "know" it is true without any doubt. My grandmother just called it "The Knowing."

Claircognizance is often hidden under the skill of precognition, but someone who has precognition only knows of future events. Claircognizance, on the other hand, precisely knows the past, present, or future. Precognition is often not so precise.

Throughout history and cultures, people with claircognizance have been called a seer, a truth-teller, a walker of two worlds, shamans, soothsayers, and much more. I was in my forties when I learned the word *claircognizance*, and researching it provided clarity and support because it was a real skill other people experienced too.

PRECOGNITION

Precognition can only be validated in retrospect, meaning after the fact. Precognition has been defined as having feelings about or seeing future events. The breakdown of the word is *pre,* meaning "in advance" and *cognition* meaning "knowledge." Precognition can both assist in developing claircognizance and coexist with it as a separate skill. For example, let's say you have a bad feeling about something, and you back out of it. Then because of reason and doubt you change your mind or get persuaded to do it anyway. Only later do you discover your gut feeling was right and you should not have done that. That gut feeling is both precognitive and claircognizant in nature. It is the same gut feeling often associated with intuition. This feeling can also be nudges from other skills. As explained in the section on intuition, this "nudge" you physically feel is your mind triggering your body to notify you. These nudges need attention and validation.

Precognition Exercise

For one month, on pieces of paper write down the events you have a strong feeling will happen and put the paper in a jar or bowl. At the end of the month, read what you wrote to see how accurate you were. Keep a journal of all your predictions. You never know how long it will take for them to come true.

TELEPATHY

We all equate telepathy with the reading of minds, which it is, but telepathy is also the sending and receiving of perceived information.

Telepathy has no visual or feelings involved. It is just bare information sent back and forth. The feelings and perceptions some get with it are from how the receiver interprets the received information. Those other senses can also be from other psychic skills. If you are a person who cannot visualize well or at all, telepathy may work for you. Telepathy skills work well with psychometry, any of the mantic arts, healing, and counseling of any type.

In her book *Telepathy*, Sybil Leek described telepathy as radio waves, and it is these mental waves you pick up on. The fact that telepathy works also confirms that thoughts are things. An example of telepathy that sticks in my mind is when my husband was thinking of selling his trailer house. I had been gone all day and when I arrived home Mike said, "Guess what?" Without hesitation, I said, "Marty is buying your house." I had no visuals, but I heard it clearly in my mind. Mike just looked at me stunned. I had no idea he had talked to Marty about the house at the time. In his excitement, he was broadcasting loud and clear. I took the words right out of his mouth, which robbed him of his excitement.

This brings us to another point of ethics and living with psychism. Sometimes, even if you know, it is better to let folks express themselves so they can genuinely experience their moment.

Telepathy Exercises

There are many telepathic skill building games. Many of them were developed in the 1960s and '70s when extrasensory perception (ESP) was the latest thing.

Sit with a friend back-to-back; have your friend choose an event with someone they are emotionally connected to, such as a child or pet they are close with. Both of you need to relax, let go, and put down any barriers. Your friend needs to keep the event clearly in their mind like they are living it. You need to relax and step aside into the deeper darkness of your subconscious, listen, and be open to receive.

Another exercise is to visit a busy place, such as a bar or grocery store, and get comfortable. As you look around, relax and tune in using the scanning skills to see if you can hear what people are thinking. A bar works especially well for this exercise because folks are letting down their guard.

When I was younger and before I knew how to push others' thoughts from my mind, I had to wear a leather jacket with the collar up against the back of my neck. This kept others' thoughts out so I could hear my own thoughts clearly. Learning to distinguish between what were my thoughts and what were not allowed me to push other people's thoughts back. After a lot of practice, that is my default filter. Now, to use telepathy I must choose to use it with intent.

Sensing is the first step in that process. I sense the person to see how open they are, and what they are broadcasting. If they are not broadcasting, I do not pry. I leave them to their privacy.

When a person says something and the other responds with "I was just going to say that!" that can be telepathy or familiarity.

FAMILIARITY

Familiarity is knowing a person very well and then discerning information about them through body language, the look on their face, how they are dressed, or knowing their habits.

I have seen familiarity used to dismiss psychic skills. However, reading the exterior of a person can be a useful tool to trigger your psychic skills. People watching is fun and useful to a psychic. Many of the exercises here involve people watching as a practice to prime the mind.

GLAMOUR AND ENCHANTMENT

Glamour and enchantment are a psychic form of hypnosis. To enchant an individual, the psychic begins with the eyes to enter the individual's consciousness. The psychic uses allure to catch their attention and spark enticement. The psychic then uses their tone of voice, hypnotic movement, and touch to excite the individual's senses to cast the glamour.

This sets the stage for the individual to believe they are part of the moment the psychic is casting. I say *casting* because I see enchantment much like casting a spell but using psychic ability rather than the typical magical spell we often construct.

In enchantment, the psychic fully needs to become the enchantment too, much like in aspecting. Living the enchantment and casting take a lot of energy for the psychic. I typically use enchantment in a romantic relationship, for sex, or in ritual. I also use it out on the astral when I find myself in an interesting situation.

Glamour

Glamour is different from enchantment in that it is a shorter-lived event. In glamour, the psychic starts, as in enchantment, with the eyes to tap into their psyche and implant the glamour. Glamour is more of a momentary distraction and can be used to get a person to momentarily change their minds.

In my twenties, I was in a pool tournament. I am not a great player and I typically played against men. So I used glamour to distract them from their best game. During one such game, I began by touching the side of the pool table alluringly. When I caught his eyes and he was fully distracted by me, I used telekinesis to push the eight ball into the pocket and he lost. He did not know the eight ball had moved until he heard it drop. I had not, however, figured out ethics yet; being ethical is especially important when using such skills.

INVISIBILITY

Believe it or not, invisibility is a very real thing and something many people do without noticing. Like flying, there are levels to invisibility and the most common is making yourself unnoticeable in a room full of people. Some people call it hiding, or withdrawing, or not paying attention, but when you are in a room full of people and no one notices you, you are effectively invisible. Many of us do this while walking down the street every day, no matter where we are or what we are doing. It is precisely this act that is the basic skill needed for invisibility.

Glamour, enchantment, and stepping aside are the precursor skills needed for invisibility because it is a matter of convincing others that they do not see you.

This is accomplished by dampening all your vibrational frequencies, which many already do inadvertently, and which is the act of intentionally withdrawing, hiding, or not wanting to be seen. Dampening your vibrations puts you in an altered state where you stop broadcasting any energy. With only dampened energy being broadcast from you, there is nothing that catches anyone's attention. You are invisible to them. Their eyes may see you, but their brain will not acknowledge the sight of you without the stimulation of vibration emanating from you.

Invisibility Exercise

Find a busy place such as a coffee shop, park, hotel lobby, or busy street. Place yourself in a prominent place that cannot be missed such as in the center of the room. For the first ten minutes or so, keep your head up. Look at people and smile or nod as they pass. See if they notice you and make a subtle point to be noticed. Then for the next fifteen minutes, put your head down and look at your phone or even just your feet. You will begin to feel the energy change. You will feel a space around you grow quiet like a bubble growing around you. Now look up and look around. Notice how the people walking by no longer even look in your direction. You are now invisible.

Scientifically, invisibility can be explained as blocking the light from being seen by another person. I have my doubts if you can actually make another not see light or if we can bend light to our favor. However, we can use glamour and enchantment skills to will a person not to see us. Practicing this allows you to be invisible at will with a thought in the real world. This skill will carry over to the astral or in trance and is not far removed from you being invisible during an OBE.

As part of an initiatory exercise, I was required to trance on the realm of the Element of Air. In Hermetic practices, the East, Realm of Air, is the angel Raphael's domain. I usually trance indoors so I am not disturbed, but for this one I sat outside. As I sat, I focused on the Element of Air. I focused on my breathing and the breath of life. I kept the focus until I could feel the air as it was absorbed by my skin. In trance, I lifted myself skyward to the place of dawn. When I arrived, Raphael greeted me. As it happens, I have issues with angles, so I was dubious about our meeting. However, Raphael was quite gracious, and I relaxed.

He offered me a drink from his flask of healing and asked what I wanted to know. I told him I wanted to explore the Realm of Air. He turned and opened the way with a wave of an arm and we walked among the clouds and mists. I remember being surprised there were no trees or mountains. He smiled and said, "This is the Realm of Air, there are no earth elements here." He showed me the rest of the realm as we talked. Soon I felt a presence come up behind me. I looked, and while I knew something was there, I could not see it. I focused more and was finally able to see something of an energy signature. It looked like heat waves coming off a car. Raphael explained that it was a Sylph, and this is their realm.

The Sylph took me farther into the realm, where other Sylphs were gathered. I watched as their energy signatures disappeared and then reappeared. I inquired about this and the Sylph said there is invisibility in all realms. The group of them then demonstrated, and the Sylph I was with explained that invisibility was a type of focused meditation. They did this until their very cells and energy signatures were transformed and could no longer be seen.

This experience gave me skills to use in the beyond and added to my skill in invisibility here on Earth, and they have proved very useful.

Chapter 6
THE MANTIC ARTS AND MORE

The mantic arts are vast and loosely defined as using objects and symbols to divine an answer or the future. Mantic arts have been used over thousands of years to predict, guide, settle disputes, and deal with personal issues. In the past, people used whatever objects were at hand to practice the mantric arts.

There are over three hundred known mantic arts; below are the ones I have experience with.

ASTRAGYROMANCY

The casting of lots, bones, runes, dice, coins, or any object that has differing sides for divination.

This may be one of the oldest and widest forms used in the mantic arts. I have made my own set of "lots" from shells and rocks, and I also have purchased a set of runes and I Ching sticks; all of those are used in astragyromancy. To use them, you cast the objects and then divine them from the symbols they reveal.

BIBLIOMANCY

I call this *book divination* and it is one of my favorites. Bibliomancy is defined as using a sacred book to get answers. Typically, it is defined as using the bible; however, I use bibliomancy with any book of my choosing.

Bibliomancy Exercise

Stand in front of your bookshelf and use the pause to clear your mind and focus on a question or topic. Then wave your hand across the bookshelf and say "reveal" as a command.

Move your hand across the bookshelf and feel for the book that is wanting to reply. This is much like running your hands over a card or rune. When the book replies, loosely hold the spine in your hand and thumb across the pages, gently blow on them, and let them fall open where they may. That is where you will see your message. I rarely have been disappointed in the messages given to me when I use this form of divination, and it is often a clearer message than what I get from the tarot cards.

CARTOMANCY

Cartomancy is divination using cards. This includes, but is not limited to, the tarot and regular playing cards. Cartomancy is about what the symbols and images on the cards invoke in your intuition and then divining meaning from them that is useful to you or another person.

Cartomancy Exercise

For this exercise, you will need a deck of tarot cards. If you are buying one, find a deck that speaks to you. Ask if you can open the box or if there are open boxes so you can look at the cards and get a feel for them.

Study each card in detail. As you look at them, write down what the symbols invoke in you. Does the Fool look like he is in danger or is he having a good time? What does the white rose on the Death card's flag mean to you? Journaling about such details is the best way to put the symbols into your memory for later use.

I have two main ways I lay out the tarot. For personal use, I normally use a three-card draw. If I want more information or I am reading for someone else, I lay out four rows of four cards. The first card in the top row going across is the past, the next is the present, then future outlook, and possible outcome. I typically read this row to the client first, separate from the rest of the spread. This row usually contains their most pressing concerns.

When I read the entire spread, the top row becomes the past. The second row is present concerns, the third row is how it is turning out currently, and the last row is the possible outcome.

CRYSTALOMANCY

This is scrying by crystal ball. When I divine by crystal ball, it usually involves trance with my eyes open. I get in a trance then open my eyes to see what the crystal ball reveals. I used to get into a trance while staring at the ball but that produced cloudy results for me. So I changed methods when reading for someone else.

Sometimes for myself, I use the crystal ball to take me into a trance. For this method, I hold the crystal and focus on it with my eyes open and begin to shift my consciousness. Then I close my eyes and continue to focus on the crystal ball while seeing it with my clairvoyance and travel deep down into the crystal until I arrive in a trance state.

DACTYLOMANCY

In dactylomancy, a tripod is placed on a basin or board that has the alphabet on it and you place your fingers on the tripod and the tripod moves by itself to spell out the answer. In other words, you use a Ouija board.

Over the years, many good and bad things have been written about the Ouija board. It is stunning to think that it was promoted to the public as a child's game in the 1960s, but it has been around much longer than that. What most fail to remember is that the board is like a séance, and like a séance, it needs to be done properly or things go wrong.

To begin, center and shield the entire room and everyone in it. The board needs you to be specific about who you want to speak to. It is important to tell the board that no one else but who you seek may enter the open space and use the planchette or anyone else in the room. Otherwise, it may cast into someone else sitting in the room who may not be prepared. I watched that happen one night as a spirit began to present in a person in the room while two other people had been expecting a reply. As sentry, I saw it happening and stopped it by interrupting.

The use of the Ouija board takes patience as spirits do not typically come forth in mere moments. When they do come forth, spirits come to anyone open to receiving them, even when a person is not aware they are open. This can leave an individual with an unexpected and unwanted experience, which is why specifics are recommended. It is also advisable to have one person sitting outside of those gathered, the sentry, to watch everyone in the room and take notes of what the board reveals. The other important, and most left out, part of using a board is to close when done. You need to send all spirits happily back to their realms, then ground and center. It is advisable to check in with everyone afterward to see how they are feeling. You are looking to see if any residuals have been left behind.

The Ouija board is a serious skill and should be taken seriously for all involved, especially the spirit being called forth. A spirit should only be called forth with consent, consideration, and respect.

HYDROMANCY

Hydromancy is divination by water in its many forms. This includes scrying in a bowl, rain, the seas, or any form of water. I and some I know will immerse themselves in water to divine or trance. I have used hydromancy with drinking water, in the shower and bath, with a hose, even a basin of wash water.

Water is an amazing element that is cleansing, transformative, and restorative. Scrying in a dish of water is much like using a crystal ball. You get into an altered state and then look deeply into the water for a reply.

LAMPADOMANCY AND PYROMANCY

These are divination by looking into a flame. This can be any flame, including from candles, a fire, or a torch. For this skill, you trance on the flame with your eyes open as with a crystal ball.

LYNCHOMANCY

Lynchomancy is divination with three lighted candles set up in a triangle. I use this form of divination for meditation and trance. As I light them, I name each candle: purity, clarity, and focus.

I use lynchomancy to divine with the three Fates. I name each Fate as I light the candles. Then I sit back and trance with them to get the information I require. To divine with the divine feminine, I name each candle the maiden, mother, and crone before dropping into a trance. Such divinations have taken me to see Cerridwyn, the Goddess Danu, and more.

ONEIROMANCY

Oneiromancy is dream interpretation. Although many of us interpret our dreams, oneiromancy is the use of dreams to divine one's future or needed guidance. This mantic art falls under dreamwork (see chapter 8). It also includes the hypnopompic and hypnogogic states of dreaming, where substantial information is received for one's betterment and guidance.

KINETIC SKILLS

The mantic arts are about using an object to divine information, and they can be quite effective. However, there are many other psychic skills the psychic can use, including the kinetic skills and automatic writing. These are advanced psychic skills rather than divinatory, so let's take a closer look at them.

Psychokinesis

Psychokinesis refers to the mental influence of physical systems and objects using only mental force. This can be almost anything, including getting a person to open a door. You can change a traffic light, or make a driver move out of your way in traffic.

When I was sixteen years old, my mom gave me a book on metapsychometry. That book clearly described me and my abilities. It gave me confidence in my skills and led me to discover I was better at psychokinesis.

With psychokinesis, you can get someone to turn around to look at you, get doors opened and elevators held, or even find a parking spot. I use it often while driving to move cars out of my way, or to stop someone in their tracks with a look.

The phrase "These are not the droids you are looking for" comes to mind. That phrase from a Star Wars movie demonstrates how psychokinesis is a combination of telepathic and kinetic action. Simultaneously, you implant the thought and the action, which compels someone to respond.

While driving, I simply look at a car and visualize it moving while I say out loud, "Move!" It is a focused command combined with mental force and the image of what I want them to do. I have about a 75 percent accuracy rate with this technique.

Telekinesis

Telekinesis refers to the movement, reshaping, or levitation of physical objects using only mental force.

In movies, we typically see the psychic in a fit of rage or crisis when using telekinesis or psychokinesis. While these emotions narrow the focus and increase the intensity of these skills, the psychic is not limited to just those times to use these skills. That said, being able to use these skills with a mere thought depends on the amount of practice you put into them. It is possible to naturally develop these skills, but further training and control is recommended.

While I do not think that someone can move an airplane as in the movie *X-Men*, I do know telekinesis and psychokinesis are real. In the example from the section on glamour, I used telekinesis to move a pool ball. I have also closed doors, heated cold pans, knocked over books, and moved many other objects.

Kinetic Skills Exercise

Put some water in a small, shallow bowl or plate and place a small leaf on top of the water. Wait for it to settle down and stop moving, then put it under a glass. Use the pause meditation to relax and gain your focus. When you are ready, concentrate on the leaf and try to get it to move. Try this exercise using a compass too.

Another exercise is to light a candle and try to get the flame to flicker. With your mind, you can change the size of the flame and even its color.

A fun exercise at a party is to put a small piece of folded paper on the tip of a pin. Put a glass over it and try to get the paper to spin.

As you progress in practice, try closing doors, tipping over books, and making a ball roll across the floor. When you are good at these, try bending a spoon.

Developing the amount of mental focus it takes to master the kinetic skills proves very useful in Magic and Witchcraft. That level of mental skill improves the outcome of all magical and energy work. In the next section, you will see how automatic writing connects with channeling skills.

AUTOMATIC WRITING

Automatic writing, or psychography, is a psychic skill where the psychic produces written words without consciously writing.

Some studies suggest that the words written arise from the subconscious; others suggest it is a spiritual or supernatural source like in channeling. Still other studies suggest automatic writing is a psychological method of tapping into the psychic's unconscious mind. All these are true of automatic writing because it can be done in any of these altered states.

An etheric being I channel is Fable; she is where my experience in automatic writing began but it did not stop there. I have written in full trance. I have written while sleepwalking, and I have written while semiaware.

Automatic writing differs from freestyle writing. In freestyle writing, you are fully conscious and freely writing down your thoughts. However, writing freestyle is how you begin to learn automatic writing.

Automatic Writing Exercise

Get comfortable with a pen and paper. Sit so you can easily write on the paper without looking at it. Take several deep breaths and relax like you are getting ready to meditate. Begin with the pause skill and work up to the first level of darkness in the stepping aside skills you mastered. With eyes closed, be calm and sense. If a sense, thought, or image comes to you, write it down without looking. Keep your hand loose. What your writing looks like does not matter; it does not matter if you are in the lines either. Let your brain communicate directly with your hand, step aside, and let it happen.

When I sit down to scribble and let my thoughts just come, that is freestyle writing. When Fable and I write, I am in a semi-aware state. Sometimes it is like arguing over the hand and what gets written. But I can mentally ask questions and get answers. It is a matter of getting into a relaxed flow. Being versed in meditation and pathworking helps this process. Give it a try and see what you come up with.

Chapter 7

WORKING WITH SPIRITS AND DEITY

Working with spirits and deity is a vast topic and a varied skill. However, there are some clear methods that hold true through time. The number one thing I see when researching this topic is most people, past and present, begin working with spirits and deity by making an effort to attract a spirit or deity. This means researching what the spirit or deity likes and then making an altar for them and putting offerings on that altar. It is best to do this research first and learn their stories in history. This way, you can tell if a spirit or deity that has presented is actually the one you were seeking and not someone or something else.

You can create your own exercise to practice working with a spirit or deity by seeking them out in meditation, pathworking, through dreams, or out on the astral. Almost all spirits and deity encounters occur in a UPG, so let's explore what a UPG is.

UNVERIFIED PERSONAL GNOSIS

Gnosis is Greek for "knowledge." Unverified Personal Gnosis (UPG) refers to an experience that is spiritual in nature. It is one that helps clarify or add information to a person's spiritual beliefs but cannot be verified by known mythology. A UPG can take many forms, including a trance, gut feeling, sudden revelation, dream, epiphany, or any form of a psychic or spiritual event.

A UPG can fill in the gaps that spirituality sometimes leaves. It is not something you make up or something you think is true. Rather, it is something you believe or know is true because you had the experience, and you trust the source or event even though you cannot prove it in any way. The majority of what occurs in Magic, psychism, and the beyond is considered a UPG.

5/11/2016

I had been working with the Goddess Hecate for a month or so, and one night when I addressed her as a Goddess, she got angry and said, "I am no Goddess I am a God!" She went on to explain that the suffix "dess" added to the end of the word God, in her time and language implied a lesser deity. She went on to explain that she was one of the original Titans and that Zeus had allowed her to keep her full powers.

The next day, I did what research I could to verify the information Hecate gave me. In all my research I only found one reference that mentions Hecate being an original titan but nothing anywhere else. Such is the nature of UPGs and working with spirits.

SPIRITS

Clarifying the words *spirit* and *spirits* is not easy because sometimes they can mean the same thing depending on how the words are used. Dictionaries and their definitions are sorely lacking and have a vast difference in opinion on these words' definitions. One of the definitions I came across is "spirits are powerful, independent entities that resist human efforts to define them." Which is vague, but also true. However, once we begin to work with them, we discover that spirits are an undefinable form without form, yet they are all forms.

No matter how familiar spirits become to us as we work with them, we find they are never commonplace and they are anything but ordinary or predictable.

Spirit forms include fairies, demons, djinns, devas, dybbuks, dankins, nymphs, mermaids, angels, elves, dragons, and so much more. Some people feel that even Gods and Goddesses are spirits, but they are something very different and you know that once you work with them.

Some believe that spirits are the messengers for the divine and they sometimes are, but they have their own agendas too. The point is, when they let us see them, it is from a realm other than our own.

Spirits have always been important to people. Enheduanna, the oldest known author, composed hymns to the Goddess Inanna more than four thousand years ago, which shows humans have been venerating spirits for a very long time. The subject of spirits is still very prevalent in our society today. Spirits are part of our growth and awareness of the world around us. Spirits create and maintain the universe. They hang the sky and the moon; they are the sky and moon. A spirit of some kind created us, and spirits have traveled with us from our earliest days.

Spirits journey through life with us and accompany us every step of the way. We would have a gaping hole within us and in life if spirits were suddenly no longer there. They are our connection to the higher purpose that gives our lives and spirituality meaning.

There has never been a time when a substantial number of people did not consider the presence of spirits to be part of normal reality, nor a time when people and spirits did not communicate and interact with one another, not even in Christianity. Working with spirits is a shared universal experience. Every group of people on Earth have some history of spiritual interaction, whether they acknowledge that interaction or not.

We have never been alone. People have not connected with spirits for thousands of years because they have nothing better to do. They do it because it produces insight, edification, and immeasurable satisfaction. Spirits are among the universe's true sacred beings. Spirits challenge axioms of space, time, and reality. Some mysteries of the universe defy human comprehension, yet some people feel there is no mystery to the working of spirits—they simply are. These people acknowledge that spirits are valid beings from the other side that come to help, and spirits are to be venerated. To those folks, what spirits do and why is not questioned; they simply have faith. Spirits are alive in their own way. No existing word may accurately express the ways in which they are alive, what they mean to you, or how they inspire you.

How did humans learn to work with spirits? Was it just born out of imagination or inspiration; or did it begin with a thought and what inspired that thought? The idea had to start somewhere, and I believe spirits inspired us to that thought. Spirits have been coming to us in inspiration and dreams for a very long time and it is through this manner they continue to communicate with us.

Spirits usually show themselves in dreams or astral travel. Typically, the first time you experience them it is in a subtle way like in a dream. Once you have developed a relationship with them, you then are better able to see and hear them while awake. To do this you must be still, let go, and listen, with your pause and scanning skills. However they appear, they are sacred beings of spirit and energy. When a spirit wishes to reveal itself, it usually does so in a form we can understand. After a time, you will be able to tell them apart: their voice or image will be different, the very feel or sensation of them will be different. That said, there are no hard and fast rules when working with spirits.

Working with a Spirit Exercise

For this exercise, we will use the spirit of someone you know who has passed. Choose someone you had a good relationship with. You can even choose a loved pet that has passed on.

Set your space and seat yourself comfortably. Begin with the pause meditation and work through a meditative state until you are in the light trance state of pathworking. Using the visualization skills, clearly visualize the person or pet. Keep the focus until the person or pet feels present. Then step aside and let the vision or experience take the lead. They will let you know when you are done.

There are many paths to the spirits. They approach us, and we approach them for a variety of reasons. A previously silent spirit may appear to help us through the next phase or obstacle for reasons of their own that they may never reveal.

How one works with spirits is an individual endeavor. Some people may adore a spirit; some may have incredible respect for a spirit or perceive it as a role model. Some people see spirits as a symbol of courage, fortitude, or generosity, and they desire the presence of the beloved entity or spirit.

Sometimes people have a special place to commune with a spirit. While in this place or moment, solutions to problems just pop into our heads. Maybe the spirit offers advice or gives warnings. However it manifests, it is communion with a spirit.

GUIDES

Guides can come to us in many ways and in many forms, so it may be hard to tell if something is a guide or not.

When I was six or so, my guide Manus began to appear in my dreams. I suddenly became aware of a man who was following me in my dreams. When I would turn and look at him, he would freeze until my attention turned away.

The next time this happened, I got a clear impression he was surprised I saw him and that I was not supposed to notice him. This made me feel he was being sneaky and up to something. Each time I saw him he was closer; he even tried to talk to me once. Scared, I finally told my mom and this is when she told me I could control my dreams. She told me to listen to him before deciding he was bad. The next dream I saw him in, he came running over a hill in a war-torn area I was in. He chased off a bad influence in the dream and told me he was my guide and so the relationship began.

We all have guides—even some we are not aware of. Some guides walk with us our entire lives but remain behind the veil or in the beyond and never reveal themselves to us.

Before we are born, a guide and our soul family agree to join us in our travels. They assist us in carrying out the challenges of our soul's path. Usually, we have known our guides and soul family before through past lives. They are like old friends and companions from a long voyage. When we meet them again after death, we recognize their presence and remember all the times they served us as we stumbled through the world.

Have you ever heard the voice of a deceased loved one or suddenly seen their face? This is known as an ancestral guide event, and not a coincidence or a matter of "I was just thinking about them." They came because they had something to say to you. That sense that someone is with you is a spirit guide.

Guides can be found in many places, and they will work through people as well. We too can be the hands, tools, mouths, servants, and messenger of spirits, guides, and deities. We are not always aware of this when this happens. Occasionally, we become aware that the spirit is working through us. Sometimes this manifests as hearing the perfect words from a friend that reach us when nothing else has. This is the entity working through them to reach me. The next time you are expecting a response from a guide, do not forget the human factor. You may be surprised by what you see and hear.

Our guides live at a different vibration than we do. To be in close contact with them may stimulate a lot of emotion. However it occurs, there comes a moment when you cross a threshold as you work with guides and spirits. Once you cross that threshold, you become more comfortable in your work with them. When they come near, it can bring to the surface the things in us that need healing or highlight our inner shadows. This is because their mere presence can heal us and enrich our lives. They can show us what we are afraid of, or what to work on next. They can show us what course of action to take to heal ourselves, what job to take, and so much more. They seek to help by empowering you to find your answers. You have only to ask; they may tell you more will be revealed or nothing, but you can ask.

Working with spirits does not mean surrendering your free will. You are responsible for your actions. If your request goes unanswered, there may be a bigger lesson to be learned, one you must do on your own. Life is full of growing pains and harsh lessons. You can also say no, when a spirit or deity comes to work with you.

Sometimes it takes pain and hardship to make us live up to our potential. Sometimes it is our destiny to experience that which we would rather never know. Knowledge acquired from pain and disappointment may turn out to be necessary and valuable. Spirits are more far-sighted than we are, and if there is no answer at all then it may not be time for us to know.

As you build a relationship with your guides, you will have fewer barriers. Fewer barriers between you and the spirit certainly, but also fewer barriers in life. Healing the emotional self is the best preparation you can do to get started working with guides.

Attracting a Guide

To begin attracting a guide, perform the activity that calls to you, whether it be reading, sewing, hiking, talking to others, or recreating. As you do the activity, loosely look for signs, stay aware, and ask the universe to bring your guides into your awareness. Look for the signs in the world around you to let them help guide you.

Guides approach when you are not really looking at them or for them, so be still, listen, and use your senses. Working with spirit guides takes commitment and dedication, and they look for that in you before they approach.

WORKING WITH DEITY

Working with a deity is different from working with a spirit or a spirit guide. Deities feel and present differently right from the start and are very clear about who and what they are. There is no vagueness about them or their intent. Their presence is tangible and impactful. Occasionally, however, a general entity will present as a deity when it is not. If you have mastered the previous skills, you will be able to tell them apart.

Attracting a Deity

To begin, choose a deity you wish to work with and research them. Find out the colors and smells they like, the food or drink they like. Research their story in history and what they are known for. Then figure out what would entice them to work with you. They are Gods; they do not just sit around waiting for us humans to say, "Hey, come here and do what I want you to do." If we said that to someone in our world, we all know the response. So we need to entice deity to want to come work with us, if they have not come seeking us as they sometimes do.

To attract a deity, place their favorite things on an altar, make offerings, and petition or worship them daily until they decide to answer. Understand that you can ask them to come work with you, but it does not mean they have to comply. Nor do they always present in a manner to our liking.

I had been exploring my connections to the Fae through dreamwork. I had a dream where being a child of the oak was significant. I tried to discover if being a child of the oak was a real thing. During my weeks of research, Hecate, whom I had worked with many times, came to me and said, "Seek the Fae." Then my spirit guide also came and told me to seek the Fae. With the message now clear, I sought out the Fae Goddess whom I had visited many times before while pathworking. The following journal entry is my experience with her.

1/4/17

The ethereal home of the Fae Goddess is a place that has all four seasons present at all times. Each season is like a different realm. I typically arrive on a moonlit winter night where a horseman jumps over a snowbank in a bluster. He then guides me along the path through the four seasons. Typically, once I get to the spring meadow I get to speak to the Goddess.

It was not so this time. When I arrived, it was a bleak winter night without snow or moonlight. This was unsettling. I had to call for the horseman. When he did arrive, he just quietly appeared behind me startling me even more.

He asked what I wanted, and I told him I was here to learn about the children of the Oak. He pointed to the path which was unusually dark and formidable and I felt trepidation I had never felt here before. I am used to seeing shadow people running alongside the path as I journey. They seem to be hunched over like Neanderthals and follow along and watch me. This time, one noticed me at the same time I noticed it and it walked up onto the path and stood before me. Suddenly, the horseman pulled up between us and asked me, "What do you want of them?"

"To respectfully know them and no longer fear them," I replied. The horseman withdrew. In the silent darkness, the shadow person and I gazed at each other. I was scanning to see what I should do next and I noticed I had no fear. So I told the creature, "I do not fear you old one, and I mean you no harm." I felt a sense of relaxation from the creature and it straightened to its full 8 ft height.

"What do you wish of me?" it asked.

"Only to know you," I replied.

Through telepathic clairvoyance, the shadow person showed me its creation. It revealed that the shadow people are the original people from the chaos. Manannan brought them out of chaos with him and they are now Manannan's watchers. They are how Manannan knows all. Then it slowly walked off the path and I proceeded.

The next thing I know I am in the spring meadow with the Fae Goddess. It is a beautiful spring day with plants all around and some of them are talking. I ask the Goddess about the children of the Oak and she says, "You must seek Manannan and the Morrigan then return to the Oak from which you come." Then I was released.

The oak from which I come can only mean the oak trees I spent so much time in as a child. The Morrigan? Well, books here I come. That research led me to the Celtic sea god (you can learn more about him in *The Biography of the Irish God of the Sea* by Charles W. MacQuarrie).

The following journal entry is my experience with him.

1/9/17

I sat before a low altar in trance seeking Manannan mac Lir, the Celtic God of the Sea. I was transported to a beach. It was a moonlit night and the sea was stormy. I looked out on the sea and felt beckoned to come forth. As my eyes searched the sea, I saw an old boat floating some distance away. I considered using it to travel to Manannan. However, I decided to jump into the sea.

I swam out and was met by a group of Undines, who are the Elemental spirits of Water. I was filled with child-like awe at their beauty and overjoyed at the honor of being allowed to swim with them. However, my joy quickly changed to fear as their temperament changed and became aggressive. I no longer felt safe and supported and stories of tricky mermaids flooded my mind as the sea whipped angrily.

Full of fear, the image of the boat came to mind and I swam toward it. As I grabbed the boat I tried to pull myself up over the edge but kept slipping. While struggling to get in the boat a hand reached out and pulled me in. It was Manannan.

"Why did you jump into the water?" he asked.

"To be in your realm instead of my own," I replied.

"Not many pass the test to reach me as you have. You knew the dangers of the Undines and the sea and still, you came. What is it you seek?"

"To know the origins of the spirit within me," I replied. He told me the Tuatha Dé Danann were my people and told me their stories of creation and war. Then he released me.

This story of my research and pathworking with deity shows how different their contact and presence can be from working with a spirit in general. There are many ways to work with spirits and other entities that are different from working with a deity, and we explore those in this next section.

THE VEIL

To me, the veil and the beyond are distinctly different. The veil tends to be more of a place of ancestors, ghosts and spirits, and etheric beings that once lived on Earth. Beyond the veil is where psychics practice necromancy, mediumship, and so much more.

NECROMANCY AND MEDIUMSHIP

Necromancy and mediumship are vast subjects to be sure and each person has their own definition and ways they work. I have boiled down my research to this: Necromancy is working with the dead and involves bringing forth a type of physical form that can be seen through séance, ritual, or ecstatic acts. Mediumship is contacting the spirit by the employ of psychic ability, with no apparition. In mediumship, we commune with the deceased and I have often wondered if mediumship fell under the category of necromancy. By this definition, it clearly does not.

In mediumship, calling forth a spirit to divine information from can be done by using an item that the desired spirit once owned. You can also gain access to the spirit through the memories and emotions of the person inquiring. Sometimes, all it takes is for the medium to think of, or call to, the person they desire to speak with. It is possible for acts of mediumship to occur spontaneously.

Sometimes spirits present to those open to hearing or seeing them, whether or not they have been asked to be present and whether or not the person knows they are open to receive. The spirits know where the open doors are.

My mother and grandmother are great examples of this. One morning two years after my mom passed, I opened my eyes to see her floating next to my bed as though she too had just woken up. She was wearing her favorite pajamas. She smiled at me and said good morning. It took me a moment to figure out if I was still dreaming or not. I was not, so I said good morning back, she smiled and left. For me, it is a common thing for Mom or Grandma to appear and give advice or to educate while I am meditating. They have shown up in my dreams or during a regular day when I am busy and given me advice about what is currently going on.

Another example of mediumship occurred when I was training to be a truck driver. My instructor discovered I was a medium through our conversation and wanted to talk to his wife. She had passed a couple of years before. It was easy for him to see her clearly, which meant I could too with clairvoyance. That allowed me to easily connect directly with her spirit. However, breaking the connection was not as easy because the instructor wanted to keep the connection, so it lasted several days before I forcefully broke it.

These examples demonstrate the importance of setting boundaries in mediumship. We need to remember we are human vessels. We have needs, limits, and requirements. Spirits have lost track of that, so sometimes we must remind them. Spirits also have boundaries and limits that we must respect. Spirits don't just linger aimlessly on the other side. They have lives and work that is important too. It is taxing on them to present here, so be considerate of the needs of the spirit. It is not polite to hold them here long.

SÉANCE

One method of working in necromancy and mediumship is through séance, which can be done alone or in a group. To do séance, you must be a master at the five parts of the stepping aside skill because you almost have to cross the veil yourself while in trance to call an unknown spirit successfully.

As with the Ouija board, for séance you must cast protection for all in the room, be very specific as to whom you will allow to present or cross, and specifically state no others may cross. While in this state of deep trance, you must use your awareness to feel if this is the intended spirit. You, in this altered state, must give or deny permission to what you feel is trying to come forward.

ASPECTING

Aspecting is a combination of channeling, glamour, and enchantment. Aspecting is used mostly in ritual. It is when you take on the aspects of a deity, entity, or a spirit. You become the embodiment of them by mastering the stepping aside skill. Aspecting is a mild form of possession where you act and speak as though you are the entity. I have seen a priestess aspect an oracle or deity in ritual many times, and you can recognize that the priestess is different when they aspect.

I aspected the Goddess Sekhmet out on the astral once, and it was intense because you have to let the deity have control of your consciousness. In aspecting, you use many of the same skills you do in channeling.

CHANNELING

Channeling is when a psychic allows an etheric spirit to enter their consciousness and take over. In order to channel, the stepping aside skill is essential to allow the entity room in your consciousness.

I channel a being named Fable that came to me in 2011 to help me teach and write. When she is in the consciousness, she typically uses automatic writing. At first, she did not write well as she had never been human before. The first week of my experience with her, she got comfortable in my human body and figured out how it worked. It was so interesting to be amazed at how my own body worked. When she writes I am not present, and I usually do not remember her encounter. After a session with her, it often takes effort to figure out the meaning of what she writes.

After a month or so of writing this way, she began to speak to my mind directly and would speak to my husband. Fable spoke of folding matter to teleport through space and time. She often mentioned how telepathy was the original way humans communicated. To her, the goal is to get us back to using telepathy. Fable said that once we can communicate by telepathy we can once again take our place in the cosmos where we originally came from.

It was Fable who helped me find the words to express my own psychism. She encouraged me to break it down into step-by-step instructions so I could teach others. I often find her writing on a subject when I wake in the morning.

My experience with Fable was the beginning of this book. I did not know I was writing a book; I thought I was writing lessons or journaling. She often says, "Write what you know and speak what you know." When I'm struggling to write, I feel her presence; I step aside and the words get written on the page, but only if I am writing by hand. So now whenever I am blocked, I sit down and journal and let her come forward as needed.

Fable came to me spontaneously. It is my understanding that most who channel a being initially have a spontaneous event with their channeled entity. Mastering the art of stepping aside and trance opens you to the ability to channel or aspect. Often, practicing those skills opens the door to channeling. The practice of those skills also helps you be ready for the unexpected, which opens the door for some wonderful enlightening experiences on your journey through the world of psychism, many of which you will experience through dreams.

Chapter 8
DREAMWORK

We each have our definition of what dreams are and what part of the brain they come from. Dreams are the re-creation of the information to and from different parts of the brain that we typically do not use during daily consciousness.

Dreams nurture the mind and soul. They spiritually and non-spiritually guide the individual. While we all dream, not everyone remembers their dreams. If I go a couple of weeks without remembering my dreams, I get uneasy and edgy. This tells me that other things in my life are out of balance and need attention.

Dreams are a form of psychic energy that emanates from the guiding principle within us and enters through our subconscious mind. Dreams usually involve the present and past as a person works through issues. However, not all images in a dream have some significance to the dreamer.

Then there are psychic dreams, which can include precognition, clairvoyance, or telepathy. Dreams even can be shared between two or more people. Other dreams have past life content or are lucid. Lucid means the dreamer is aware of the dream and in some cases can direct its outcome.

Dream Exercise

Always try to meditate on any dream fragments and hard-to-remember dreams. Doing so increases your ability to lucid dream.

For this exercise, go right to your meditation space after waking up from a dream. Once in a meditative state, let yourself slip back into a near-hypnopompic state and visualize the dream you just left. This must be done in a languid state and not forced. Let the dream state take over but do not fall asleep.

Sometimes we are not meant to remember our dreams. I had a troubling dream one night and my dog woke me from it every time I went back to sleep. She would not leave me alone when I attempted to meditate on it. I figured the dream was not meant to be remembered. Sometimes we must listen to the signs; when a door closes, let it close. While dreams are a category of their own, they also fall under psychism and are a vast subject that needs some definitions applied to narrow it all down.

HISTORICAL BELIEFS ABOUT DREAMS

Throughout history, dreams were considered supernatural events that contained prophecies, predictions, divinations, and messages from the Gods. Dreams were and still are the vehicle that spirits use to communicate with humans. They certainly work that way for me, which is why I place dreams in the category of the beyond.

Dream interpretation was important to the ancient Babylonians and Greeks. Aristotle dismissed the idea that the Gods were the source of dreams. Yet the Greeks attempted to incubate healing dreams by spending a ritual night in the temple of Aesculapius, the God of healing. The focus was on the individual's dreams and the right dream meant a cure.

However, during the Middle Ages, the Church asserted itself as the ultimate authority. They believed that dreams should be ignored, which heralded the end of widespread belief in miracles and supernatural events. Even though church leaders discouraged it, dream interpretation continued. Dream interpretation was an important service that wizards and astrologers offered. Dreams became the subject of magical formulas, and various handbooks based on the work of Artemidorus were circulated.

Before the late nineteenth century, psychological explanations did not include dreams. It was psychiatrist Sigmund Freud in his pioneering work, *The Interpretation of Dreams*, who first considered dreams the road to the unconscious. He believed they were wish-full filaments of repressed desires and daytime residues, which were triggered by nocturnal releases of these repressed elements in the form of dreams.

Freud used free association to interpret dreams. In free association, the dreamer says whatever comes to mind concerning the various elements in a dream. Because of the sexual nature of Freud's psychology, elements seen in a dream were regarded as either phallic or vaginal symbols. Although many of us do not view dreams the way Freud did, we still use much of his theology about dreams today.

Later, psychiatrist Carl Jung considered dreams the expression of the contents of the unconscious. He said the purpose of dreams is to provide information about the self, achieve psychic equilibrium, and offer guidance, which is what most of us believe today.

Jung believed that dream symbols from the collective unconscious had universal or archetypal meanings but symbols from the personal unconscious do not. Those symbols take on meaning from the individual's experiences, beliefs, and cultural, racial, ethnic, and religious heritage. Jung felt that only the dreamer, not an outsider, could interpret a dream's true meaning. He considered dream interpretation of utmost importance in the process of an individual becoming whole. I agree with both of Jung's concepts and apply them to my work. (For more on Jung and dreams, see James Hall's *Jungian Dream Interpretation: A Study in Jung.)*

Dream symbols are the raw language of the unconscious, brought to the attention of the conscious unfiltered. Dreams can tell us the true state of our lives. They show us where we are in terms of what needs to be dealt with consciously. For example, symbols of the shadow self, or repressed aspects of the self, often appear in dreams. They appear to get our attention and are there for us to interact with.

According to Jung, our psyche seeks to have a dialogue with us and brings us information in three successive ways: first, psychically, as in dreams; second, through fate such as accidents or chance encounters; third, through physical disorder and illness. Jung further felt that to ignore our dreams is to court more drastic events.

Since Freud and Jung, other theories have been put forward on the nature, function, and meaning of dreams. For the most part, however, their elaborations are based on the work of these two giants.

THE NATURE OF DREAMS

In the early 1950s, research at the University of Chicago found that dreams occur during the REM sleep cycle, which they found to be crucial to the process of learning new skills.

Robert W. McCarley and J. Allan Hobson, psychiatrists at Harvard Medical School, theorized that dreams are born in the brain stem. This is where neurons using the chemical acetylcholine fire bursts of electrical signals to the cortex. This is where higher thought and vision originate. The cortex attempts to make sense of the signals by rearranging them, along with real memories, into a story or concept we can understand. Allan Hobson's *Dreaming as Delirium* has more information on the study.

In his dreamwork, Edgar Cayce would dream, wake, and write down his experiences; he did an extensive study into lucid dreaming. Today, his work continues at the Association for Research and Enlightenment Cayce Institute in Virginia Beach, Virginia. Freud observed that sleep creates favorable conditions for telepathy, and he often referred to dream telepathy in his clinical work with patients. Cayce's work clearly demonstrates Freud's observation. Dream telepathy has been of interest to psychical researchers and parapsychologists since the late nineteenth century.

The founders of the Society for Psychical Research (SPR) in London collected 149 dream telepathy cases in their study of spontaneous paranormal experiences, which was published in *Phantasms of the Living,* circa 1886. There are currently two volumes of this writing in the California Digital Library. There are about a dozen scientific demonstrations of telepathy in dreams. The most famous was research conducted from 1962 to 1974 by Montague Ullman, Stanley Krippner, and others at the Dream Laboratory of the Maimonides Medical Center in Brooklyn, New York. They later wrote a book together titled *Dream Telepathy*.

As for symbols, there are as many symbols and interpretations for dreams as there are people. Each dreamer has their own base of symbols that work for them. It is much like selecting a tarot deck that works for you; you select symbols that resonate with you.

PREDREAM STATES

The hypnagogic state is the stage of sleep between wakefulness and sleep, and the hypnopompic stage is the one between sleeping and waking. These are the two predream states.

The Hypnagogic State

The hypnagogic state is the state where you can begin to learn how to control dreams. This state shows you what it is like to be lucid, a skill that will carry over to astral travel and visions. The pre- and postdream states are a place of great insight. In them we often find spiritual communication and one of several places you can talk to your subconscious. I use the hypnogogic state differently than the hypnopompic state. The hypnogogic state, which is the presleep stage, is where I will choose a subject to dream on for dreamwork. For dreamwork, I set a topic to sleep on and think of it as often as I can as I fluctuate between sleep and lucidity. I usually wake with an answer.

Both the hypnogogic and hypnopompic states are when our daily consciousness shifts at the same time our subconscious does. During this shift, they communicate with us while we are semilucid. The *Encyclopedic Psychic Dictionary* validates this theory; it describes these two states as a short time span just before and after sleep when the conscious and subconscious minds are changing dominance in their roles. This sets up an equilibrium type of activity where the two minds are on the same level, during which the mind is receptive to sounds, images, ideas, feelings, and intuitions. The material rises from the subconscious and some of it is psychic in nature.

If dreams provide contact with spiritual and psychic forces, as Edgar Cayce said, then the hypnagogic and hypnopompic states are the gateways to those forces.

The imagery that occurs in these two states is different from dream imagery. Often, the imagery is more like fragments, but they are equally instructive to the individual. The two states are the equivalent of visual thinking, often expressed in one's own system of symbols. Interpreted, these symbols can then provide answers to questions and problems and even alert one to future circumstances and events.

Rousing oneself from a hypnopompic state to record the images is beneficial. With practice, I have developed some memory tricks that allow me to remember some of what I see in the hypnopompic state. So I no longer must wake, write, then drop back into a hypnogogic state.

Hypnopompic State Exercise

When you receive a concept or idea in the hypnopompic state, you are typically lucid. Tell yourself, "I am going to remember that" and repeat two times a sentence or word about what you want to remember. Also, keep a pen and paper next to your bed so you can write down dream fragments. This will create muscle memory in your brain and train it to begin remembering how to be lucid.

I do these exercises while still in the hypnopompic state. About 50 percent of the time, I remember with no problem. Other times, I wake thinking, "What was that I wanted to remember?" And that triggers my mind to search for it, usually with great success. I use this same method to go back into an interrupted dream.

I also have been known to get up from a deep sleep, write about ten paragraphs on a subject I have dreamed about, and then go back to sleep. After which, I either have a slight recollection or no recollection of what I have written. In my experience, it is possible with applied awareness to extend the lucidity of the hypnopompic state by choosing to drop back off to sleep for a moment.

THE DREAM STATE

A dream state is the activity of the mind during sleep that is between the lower beta and upper alpha levels. The dream state is a level of consciousness during sleep where a person's mental activity is busy producing visions of people and scenery. This occurs along with impressions of speaking and emotions. Dreams occur at ninety-minute intervals throughout a normal night of sleep. The visions of stories or fragments in dreams last between five to forty-five minutes and increase in length toward morning. This stage displays low beta waves and high alpha waves in EEG readouts where the sleeper's eyes move rapidly under closed lids.

Dreams can present in still scenes or story form. A dreamer can dream as a subject, a spectator, or both at the same time. They can be black and white or color. In dreams, the dreamer typically understands any conversation through telepathy.

Dreamwork Exercise

Before you fall asleep, do whatever relaxes you the most. You want to be as languid as you can and able to dream. As you settle in, think of what you want an answer for repeatedly until you fall asleep. Try to make it something simple and use words such as "solve a work problem" or "fix a relationship," and think of the person. Keep with this practice; it can take a while to be successful.

Your natural sleep cycles will determine which sleep state works better for you. I fall asleep fairly fast and wake slowly. You might be a person who falls asleep slowly and wakes fast, or goes slowly or quickly through both states. With practice, it is possible to accomplish either and use it to your benefit. Practicing this takes time and effort. So start with what occurs naturally and work from there.

In the hypnagogic state, astral travel is more likely, and in the hypnopompic state, visions, OBE, and clairvoyance are more likely. I suspect this is because in the latter state we are coming from REM sleep and in the former we are going into our deeper selves where it is easier to access our astral self.

It is while in a hypnogogic state that author and psychiatrist Judith Orloff begins her dreamwork by giving herself an image, suggestion, or question to dream on. She receives the answer when she wakes. This gives credit to the phrase "Sleep on it."

These stages are exercises for the psychic mind. They are a common place and time for natural clairvoyance to occur. If you apply awareness to this state of consciousness, you certainly can ask questions of it and expect a reply. You develop this awareness by paying attention to what impressions and other stimuli you receive while in these states. Let thoughts and images come and just observe and later journal about them.

DREAM AVOIDANCE

Dream avoidances are things we do not want to know or are not meant to bring back with us. The theory is that the symbols and scenes we see in dreams and then forget are portions of waking life that we would like to forget or evade intentionally. This makes the dreamer wake before the dream is finished.

Sometimes our dreams reveal things we are not ready to deal with or are not ready to comprehend. To do so could be harmful to our psyche, so our minds prevent this and they are avoided.

PSYCHIC DREAMS

Psychic dreams are dreams that use psychic skills or where psychic skills occur during the dream, such as precognition, clairvoyance, or telepathy. As dreams originate from our internal psyche, psychic dreams are a common occurrence even if we do not display psychic skills in our waking life.

DREAM CLAIRVOYANCE

Dream clairvoyance is a psychic experience of emotional clairvoyance happening during sleep. This is experienced while the mind is active with theta brain waves. In the theta state, there is no rapid eye movement. Dream clairvoyance is a very vivid and detailed vision that is typically easy to recall. The journal entry shows an example from one of my dreams.

7/16/2020

While dreaming, I become lucid and see my great-nephew in an outdoor setting. He is upset and walks away and sits down at a picnic table, puts his face in his hands, and says, "I tried to stop but couldn't." He was crying. I woke knowing something was wrong. However, because of my busy life, I did not contact his father for several days. When I did, his dad confirmed that is exactly how and when the events occurred.

What is remarkable about this journal entry? Although I am not overly emotionally connected to my great-nephew, I am to the father. But they live thirty-five hundred miles away and I rarely see them or have contact with them. However, this is the nature of dream clairvoyance and is typical when family members have dreams about each other.

PRECOGNITIVE DREAMS

Precognitive dreams are defined as dreams of future events regarding the self or others. Direct precognition differs in that it can occur almost any time. Precognitive dreams are a psychic experience that occurs between REM states. They often come to prepare someone for an event that is going to happen or may happen if not avoided.

The most significant precognitive dream I had was while living in Portland. In the dream, I saw a well-dressed man with a briefcase walking toward me. Suddenly, a mugger hiding in a recessed doorway grabbed him. The mugger hit the man on the head from behind. I woke in a panic because the event was so real. It took a while to settle down enough to go back to sleep.

Several months later, I was walking down the street when I was overcome with déjà vu. My body tingled all over. As I looked around, the scene was familiar in an odd way I could not place. As I stood there trying to figure it out, I saw the man in my dreams walking toward me. He was getting close to the doorway where I knew there was a mugger hiding. I yelled at him to watch out.

He ducked as the mugger swung a pipe at him and missed. We both stood there dazed and confused as the mugger ran off. The man thanked me and left. I am certain the experience was surreal for all involved.

Since then, I have kept a journal of my dreams and have documented a future car accident and much more. This demonstrates the value of journaling and shows that sometimes precognitive dreams do not leave a clear impact on our memory because we too easily dismiss them. Yet respectfully dismissing them is valid. This is because not all dreams have meaning, making quite the conundrum, and is why examining, meditating, discussing, and journaling our dreams is valuable time spent.

DREAM CONTROL

Dream control means to be lucid while dreaming and able to manipulate the outcome of what is occurring in the dream by thought or will.

When I was young, my mom taught me to control my dreams after I experienced nightmares. She said that I could bring her or any item I might need into my dreams. "They are just dreams, and there is no need to fear them," she would say. She told me that because dreams come from my mind, I could control them. In my thinking, what my mom said was true, and I had no trouble with nightmares after that.

Ever since, I have been able to control my dreams and be lucid. I had no idea what a tremendous gift she gave me until many years later. Now I use dreamwork, astral travel, and trance work and can bilocate with ease and I do so prolifically, all because of that one moment in time with my mom.

Dream control happens when you are lucid and you decide to change things in the dream by rejecting what is occurring. I was lucky because when I was little, my mom told me I could control my dreams and I believed her. Teaching yourself to control dreams takes practicing all the skills and then using them in your dreams. However, you need to know and believe you can do so. To have that kind of conviction takes practice.

In Witchcraft there is a saying, "As above, so below, As the universe, so the soul, As without, so within." This very much applies to anything that counts as the beyond and everything Magic—meaning anything you do on Earth you can do in the beyond and in Magic. Unfortunately, not everything you do in dreams or the beyond can be done here. But the principles and meanings of what occurs in the beyond are applicable here. So all the skills you learn here you can apply in the beyond.

You can do Magic and use psychic skills in dreams, out on the astral, in the cosmos, and anywhere in the beyond if you are lucid.

DREAM FRAGMENTS

Dream fragments are parts of a dream appearing by themselves or appearing unfinished. Sometimes they present as scenes that stop and start in different settings or as scattered symbols. These fragments can still be used for interpretation when the dream is not in story form or cannot be fully recalled.

Dream fragments are a type of free association your mind is doing. Ever have your thoughts just keep running while trying to get to sleep? Dream fragments are the same type of activity from your subconscious. They can still be a valid and viable source of information about everyday stresses; however, they typically do not have a psychic nature to them.

DREAMS FOR HEALTH

Dreams for health are dreams in which an individual receives directions and instructions to improve one's health. They do not fully replace clinical medical care, but often will improve your situation.

When I dream for my health, I keep my topic in mind as I fall asleep and I typically wake with useful information. Dreaming for health falls into the category of dreamwork and is done using the same skills.

Healing dreams were Edgar Cayce's expertise and he wrote many books on the subject. In his work, he could see clairvoyantly through a person's body and read their health while he was dreaming. Cayce was also called the sleeping profit (see Medical Clairvoyance).

LUCID DREAMING

Lucid dreams occur in the normal dream cycle where the dreamer is aware that they are dreaming. While lucid, you are in full possession of your waking consciousness. You are also aware that you are asleep. This sensation might be a little unsettling the first time it happens; you may feel a bit of confusion or panic. This is the time to bring your magical and psychic skills into the dream with you, use the pause and scan, and breathe through it or ground yourself.

The important thing is to relax. Breathe through it. Remember you are dreaming, let the discomfort pass through you, and enjoy the new worlds and experience you have as you begin to work in the beyond.

Chapter 9
THE BEYOND

The beyond involves a deep altered state of mind and includes UPGs, trance experiences, astral realms, portals, multiverses, timelines and timeline jumping, dreams, crossing the hedge, working in the cosmos, visions, and much more. The beyond covers all the varied things that are generally unexplainable or not labeled through common definitions of psychism, Magic, and Witchcraft. The beyond is only limited by you.

To become aware of and experience the beyond typically takes documentation of all your psychic events and practice of all the skills over a period of many years.

That said, a few folks have these things happen spontaneously without practice. We are the ones who say, "I was born like this." If you are one too and have managed your psychism well, you will know of what I speak when I say that the beyond is often unexplainable. I have prepared you for the beyond throughout this book, to help you understand the beyond when I describe some of what it contains.

ASTRAL TRAVEL

Astral travel is a phenomenon in which a person feels separated from their physical body and seems to be able to travel to, and perceive, distant locations on Earth or in non-worldly realms. It requires a relaxed state of consciousness to begin and is a technique that transpires in a conscious or unconscious state. There are many astral planes, not just one or seven but vast numbers of them, and they can be anywhere or any time period.

Astral travel is something we all do and is one of my all-time favorites. It is linked to dreaming because it typically happens when we are sleeping and seems like it is a dream, which begs the question, how do you know you are traveling rather than dreaming?

Dreams are often like watching things occur and are typically about our daily stuff. Astral travels are expansive. They include worlds and lives rather than just scenes or stories as in dreams. Also, control is more prevalent in astral travel than in standard dreaming.

In the process of astral travel, there is usually a physical sense that the body is involved. Astral travel feels more like you are living the experience. In dreams, this is not typical. We all have an astral body that lives another life on other planes. It is that body, our spirit, or maybe even part of our soul that travels. It is hard to know for sure; many think it is just part of our consciousness that travels.

Any of those are possible but think of it like this: The physical body is the clothing of your inner self. It is comfortable for the inner self to get out and leave the clothing behind. The physical body you know so well is not the sumtotal of who and what you are—it just holds your inner self.

I once had an experience where I went from a dream into astral travel and then back into the dream all while lucid. The dream part had quite a different feel to it.

While astral traveling, your survival instincts are still intact. They are more loosely defined but they are present and available. They present as fears, such as the fear of going too far while flying, or the fear of dying if you hit bottom after falling. These are the fears that keep us connected to our daily consciousness. They are not real or true but they keep us connected. This connected consciousness is the very thing that keeps us safe.

Astral Travel Exercise

This exercise is a waking exercise and designed to get you familiar with what astral travel may feel like when you are asleep and lucid.

Set your space so you will not be disturbed for at least an hour. Get seated, feet on the floor, and work the skills from pause to trance and get very relaxed.

Now with eyes closed become aware of your body, relaxed and feeling like it is asleep. Once you feel your inner etheric body, visualize it standing up. It turns and sees you sitting in the chair. This is your astral body, let it look around and take in the details of the room. Now will your astral body to walk around the place you are in. Check out all the details, look out the windows. Relax and enjoy the process.

Now let your astral body walk out the door. Look around and get a good idea of where you are and notice all the details. Now go for a walk in the area and look for something that catches your attention. (Give yourself about five minutes for this part of the exercise.) It can be a rock, flower, lawn ornament, bird's nest, color, the top of a roof, anything. Now will yourself to that object and examine it closely. Is there a sensation in your hand as you hold it?

When you are done with the object, bring yourself back to your body. Walk in the door and stand before yourself. See every detail of you as you look at your body. Now visualize your astral body facing away from you and see it sit down into your physical body. Feel it as it enters you and you merge. Breathe and relax. You now become aware of your physical self: you feel your body resting against the chair, feel your feet on the floor. Your astral body is all the way back into your physical body. You feel very relaxed; your body begins to wake up as you bring your awareness back to the here and now. Slowly come back from the altered state until you are fully awake, then open your eyes. Breathe, stretch, and relax before getting up. Make sure to ground your energy and get something to eat and drink once you come out of this working.

Many things happen on the astral that do not happen in everyday life. You can travel from one spot to the other with a mere thought. You can fly, you can go anywhere you want to. Your body seems stronger and more agile. Because it is less affected by gravity your astral body can do some amazing things.

Some people think that the astral is the real world, and this world, our body, and all this, is the illusion. Out on the astral I have been to other planets, visited the Gatekeepers, and played in the cosmos. The Gatekeepers are the cosmic beings that guard the cosmos and all it contains. As you will see from the journal entry, it is also possible to accomplish astral travel within an astral travel.

2/5/10

I woke that morning feeling like a truck had run over me. My body hurt and ached everywhere and my head was still foggy. It was like most nights going to bed and falling asleep when suddenly I was before an immense ancient door that opened just for me. As I walked in there was a Moorish man at a desk. He was surrounded by scrolls, books, and papers all over. I felt timid, as he looked up at me so, I gifted him some silver fabric. Pleased he nodded and waved me to pass to his left around the desk. Once past the desk, I noticed a grey shop front with two witches on the stoop dressed in Romany style clothing. They backed away from me as I passed so I kept to the right. Around the bend of the path to my right, there was a dark-haired woman next to a white leather reclining chair that seemed to be behind the front desk.

She motioned me into the chair and guided me out on another astral plane. I watched another part of me split and look back on the astral me laying in the chair with curiosity.

In my second astral form, I went to the grey storefront and stood before the witches on the stoop this time they opened the door for me. Once my eyes adjusted to the darkness inside, I saw a wall on my right and to my left, I began to see rows of tapestries several stories tall. Looking up I saw an odd being floating near the top and floated up to greet it. The being raised a hand and a tapestry raised and the being motioned me to go look at it.

It was the tapestry of my life and it showed me that a third man was coming into my life soon. I looked up at the being and it smiled, looking back at the tapestry I saw a journey but could not see the details. The tapestry went back in place and it was time to go. As I left, I tossed a coin to the witches on the stoop and proceeded to my body in the chair. Only the dark-haired woman stood in front of me and motioned me to another section across from her where a woman was holding on to a white horse wearing only a bridle.

She directed me to get on and lay down on its neck and close my eyes. When I did, I was again split astrally, this time into the dark of the great beyond. My third astral self-moved through several universes. Then I passed through another kind of barrier and all was still, dark, and quiet and I had a moment of alarm. Then I heard a female voice say that is beyond her limits bring her back. Visually I saw myself propelled back through the universes, through the astral self on the horse, through the astral self in the chair, and, then back into my body in bed all in one moment and quite rapidly. Kind of like being drug through a knothole at high speed.

After this event, I made sure to do my self-care and paid attention to what my body and mind needed to recover. It took me three days to feel like myself again. A week later I met my current husband and we began our journey together. I am sure this place was my version of the Akashic records. It makes me wonder if my body was painful from experiencing sleep paralysis but I was not aware of experiencing paralysis that night.

SLEEP PARALYSIS/ASTRAL CATALEPSY

Astral catalepsy is a period in which both the astral and physical bodies are stiff and nonmoving. This is sleep paralysis and occurs when the astral body first lifts out to begin its journey. Some people are scared by this experience. It is unsettling to be sure; however, I have found when I became lucid during paralysis, and I used my pause and scan skills, the paralysis would diminish; perhaps it will for you too.

I talk myself through paralysis by first looking at the facts and telling myself, "This is the onset of travel, relax, breathe, and let go." After several times of doing this, I no longer experience the paralysis, at least not in a fearful state or while lucid.

Paralysis is your body experiencing a transition from the physical to the astral and your body needs a moment to adjust while your consciousness shifts to another plane of reality. To do this, the body temporarily shuts down, which is the cause of the paralysis. If you can coach yourself through it, you will succeed in astral travel and many other threshold types of psychism. If you cannot get past the fear of sleep paralysis, it will block you from astral travel.

ASTRAL PLANES

The astral plane is the name given to the vast planes of the etheric world, of which there are many. The astral planes vibrate faster than the vibrations here on Earth and they are usually perceived clairvoyantly. The astral planes have a level of awareness in the etheric world that have their own principles, inhabitants, and purpose for existing. Here you travel by thought and though I have seen seasons, there seems to be a constant temperature. It is very easy to change forms and go from one astral plane to another with a mere thought.

A note here: It is possible to have a dream or astral clairvoyance and not have clairvoyance in the real world. However, you can tap that dream clairvoyance and bring it to the here and now with practice.

ASTRAL BODY

The astral body is an invisible ethereal substance within the physical body. I and others believe it is possible to have other forms or bodies. Astral bodies are parts of our consciousness. They are the vehicle in which we perceive or experience travel. I have a butterfly body and a cat-human hybrid body. My husband has a reptilian-human body, which I have seen when we travel together. The journal entry provides an example of astral bodies and lives from one of my experiences.

2/23/11

In this travel I become lucid in an old castle in a large room and I have students before me at a table. I feel as though I just dropped in on someone else's life and it took me a moment to figure out what to do. The students were about twelve years old and just finishing up a project. With the class done I became hungry and went to the large drafty galley to find something to eat, but it was late and there was not much left. I found a cooked crab and decided to take it back to my room.

On my way I found myself dressed in a cotton sleeping gown and wearing sandals but had one of them in my hand. I walked back through the now empty classroom and out a large exterior door, and into a torrential rain in the dark. As I struggled with the door, I dropped my food and my shoes in a large mud puddle and was now soaked to the skin. Annoyed, I crossed the courtyard and went to my room to dry off and change.

The next thing I know it was time to be back in class. I was having a one-on-one conversation with a student at the end of the table when a bunch of late teens came in and took up the rest of the table seating. They were throwing paper airplanes, being loud, knocking things over, and being unruly. I stood up (in the dream) and said aloud, "Damn brats they are no different over there than they are here!" Which woke me and my husband. He turned to me asking what was going on. When I told him I was teaching Magic to teenagers on the astral, he laughed. Astral travels can be fun or serious, you just never know.

ASTRAL REALMS

I use the term *astral realms* in addition to astral planes. Realms are the places that exist on the astral planes. Realms are complete places, not fragments of our current existence or figments of our imagination or subconscious. They are complete places with their own planets, their own multiverses or solar systems, and their own people and customs. You often can and do experience real life in these realms as you interact with who or whatever lives there, and they are not all nice.

Being lucid while traveling the realms is helpful so you can tell yourself, "Oh this is not my world, I'm safely in bed." If you cannot be lucid but still remember your travels, knowing it is another realm allows you to compartmentalize appropriately.

PORTALS

Nearly anything or anywhere can be a portal in the beyond. Some you can visually see and they look like a portal; with others, you touch something or take a step and suddenly you are somewhere else. So if you experience that while you are in the beyond, you now know it is a portal.

MULTIVERSES

The multiverse is a collection of diverse observable universes all existing next to each other. Each is composed of everything that makes up a universe as we know it. It is in these multiverses that the astral realms exist.

It is possible to visit any of them individually or all of them at once, which is enough to drive a psychic mad if not well skilled mentally. These kinds of events are why I suggest you find someone who understands multiverses and talk to them, journal a lot, and use self-care.

TIMELINES

Because there are multiverses and astral realms within each, astral realms and multiverses contain multiple timelines. I know that is a lot to wrap your head around and yes, they are infinite. Timelines are basically the trajectory our lives take as we move through time. Each realm or multiverse measures time a bit differently, so we will stick to how we measure time here in this world. In our world and reality, a timeline is the path our lives take as we make decisions and deal with those results. Most of us believe that once you are on a timeline it does not change. That is not so; you can jump from one timeline to another.

Timeline Jumping

Timeline jumping is moving from one timeline to another. This can be achieved through conscious choices that we know will drastically change our lives. Have you heard stories about people who just suddenly decide to wipe the slate of their current lives and start over anew? That is timeline jumping by choice.

More typically, a timeline changes when we survive a traumatic experience. For example, when a person in an accident miraculously survives somehow when they should have died. Afterward, their lives are very different, usually in a blessed way. That is an example of jumping a timeline due to trauma. Timeline jumping can happen from unexpected events too, not just traumatic ones. An example of that can be when you are going about the normal business of your life and an unexpected opportunity drops in your lap that completely changes your life in one single moment. Timeline jumping happens in the beyond as well.

Timeline Jumping in the Beyond

Our astral bodies also have lives that can jump timelines. We all have other versions of ourselves in the multiverses, and each of them has a timeline that can be changed. While this might be immense to think about, it is not as immense as the possibilities of the cosmos.

THE COSMOS

The cosmos do not exist on any planet or in any one multiverse or realm. Rather, the cosmos are the intelligent web of matter that holds together all that we fondly call the universe and more. Some might call it the expanse of space itself. The cosmos hold all the multiverses and all they contain. The cosmos are full of beings, life, and Magic and are where the guardians of all life in all multiverses live and do their work.

These guardians are different than the guardians that watch over the elements. These guardians watch over the cosmos and all the planets. It is possible to visit them or to do magical works with them in the cosmos on your own through trance, astral travel, or dreamwork. I have had several conversations with them by using those skills and it was usually about what is to come for Earth or what we need to do next. Working in the cosmos is truly an experience and a much grander thing than going over the hedge.

OVER THE HEDGE

Going over the hedge is different from going across the veil or going into the beyond. In my family tradition, going across the hedge means going out of this realm into another and gaining helpful information and bringing it back and using it. Going across the hedge is like a psychic dream. You will need the skills of pathworking, clairvoyance dreamwork, astral traveling, dream control, and lucidity while sleeping. To cross the hedge, you need to master all those skills and practice, practice, practice. Some folks are lucky enough to be able to cross the hedge naturally; it is a gift indeed, for others must work very hard at it.

While across the hedge, I have been instructed about herbs I am not familiar with and how to use them for someone's health and have done so successfully. While across the hedge, I have been instructed on rituals and many other kinds of healing.

In the hedge crossing described in the following journal entry, I journeyed back to a medieval village to visit Mell, a wise woman whom I have visited many times.

6/19/16

As usual when I cross over to see Mell, I arrived in the field. I so enjoy the walk up to the village. I like to gather fresh heather for Mell on the way. Today my dog Molly came with me and she was happily at my side. Molly in the real world has been sick of late, with a bad cough and I want to ask Mell about it.

My basket full of heather, we reach the village and approach Mell's Inn. When the door swings open the rich smells from her kitchen make me smile. I find her in the kitchen at the bread table. She takes the heather from me and motions for me to sit by the fire, as she hands me a bowl of stew. We chat for a while about the herbs she has gathered when Molly jumps into my lap. Mell gives Molly the eye and then says let me see her. Mell puts her on the tale and looks her over, then tells me to give her burdock in something sticky to cure her cold. We visit a bit more and then the crossing is over. When I wake, I begin researching burdock and discover it is used for respiratory issues. I decide to powder it and mix it in vegetable glycerin to give to Molly. Three days later Molly no longer had a cold. Thanks, Mell!

In another such crossing, I went to see Cerridwyn and she directed me on how to make a particular spell for someone's prosperity. In others, I have been shown how to do certain rituals. In my practice, crossing the hedge is always about healing, ritual, or Magic and bringing back useful information. Crossing the hedge is different than flying.

FLYING

Since days of old, witches have flown and there is a lot of lore written about witches flying that is not verified. This is because flying falls under UPG, unverified personal gnosis.

There are levels to flying that many of us modern witches do without even realizing. Have you ever daydreamed and just let your mind roam or zone out? Or used the wandering mind meditation? Those are the first steps to learning the needed skills in flying. They prime your brain for free association drifting, which is needed in flying.

To accomplish this, you need to put your linear mind aside, step aside, and dissociate. Thereby consciously shifting the consciousness into a different kind of altered state to one of limbo, beyond the trance level or even stepping aside. In flying, we remove mental barriers and let any state of mind come to us as it chooses in any form it chooses. In effect, it is a very deep mental state of the wandering mind meditation. My journal entry describes one of my flying experiences.

I do not recommend this kind of flying unless you are well practiced in trance, astral travel, and working with spirits, and in good health.

7/2/1017

I became lucid in the dream as I walked into a room full of students and said who wants to learn how to fly? I leaped and willed myself into the air ten feet above the students. I somersaulted, stopped in mid-air, extended my arms, and I floated there. Then I levitated the students into the air. We flew around and played in the air. When the lesson was over, I simply flew home.

That example shows naturally occurring flying events that can come in dreams and astral travel. They also can be brought on by ecstatic works such as dancing, chanting, or drumming.

Enhanced flying is a much different type of flying; for this you imbibe in a substance to aid in flying. (Please obey all laws regarding any substances and age requirements.)

This kind of flying is a hallucinatory experience and is brought on by the use of herbs and potions. To be ready for this type of flying, you must be able to distinguish between what is real and what is not, and be able to distinguish between what is valuable vision and what is nonsense. Additionally, you must develop the ability to let the nonsense flow on by and detach from it, even if it is ugly, gruesome, ridiculous, scary, or intense. Being skilled in these areas allows a small measure of control while flying enhanced.

Flying Enhancements

Caution: Recipes for flying potions and ointments are guarded like stolen gold. The main reason for this is safety. So here is the golden rule: always do your own research on any herb or oil you use.

Herbs and oils are chemical compounds like any other medicine and there can be complications even if they are listed as harmless.

Before using flying potions and enhancements that you make or purchase, your health issues and any medications or supplements you are taking must be researched to see how they will interact with each other. If you are unsure of what is in something, please do not let yourself be talked into taking it, even when a trusted friend says, "You've got to try this," or when buying it from a store. Nothing is worth risking your health or your mind.

When you are sure of the herb or oil you wish to use, there are many common and uncommon enhancements available. Below is a list of ones I have experience with.

Common Flying Enhancements

Please obey all laws and age limits regarding these enhancements.

Enhancements include cannabis, alcohol, wine, mead, and beer. Some of us are familiar with these enhancements and have achieved an altered state from their use. To experiment with flying while under their influence, lie quietly in a dark space and allow yourself to see beyond the room you are in. You can do this with your eyes open or closed. During this time, you may begin to see hallucinatory images. This method is like looking at one of those pictures of colored dots until you can see the sailboat—that is, looking without looking.

I use the above enhancements for first-level flying. First-level flying is not as intense or colorful as other levels, nor does it last as long as second-level flying done with other enhancements. However, it is by far the most common and safest.

Less Common Flying Enhancements

Caution: These herbs are commonplace but do not have common effects. Please use caution and obey all laws regarding their use. I have not been courageous enough to try the baneful herbs for flying and I do not recommend doing so. Dosing and the strength of baneful herbs can be tricky with fatal results.

The less common enhancements I have used are hallucinatory mushrooms, DAP, yohimbe bark, damiana, and mugwort. All of which are legal where I live.

For flying, I smoke these herbs because I have more control with dosing and effect. Several companion herbs can enhance the effect of those listed above. They are white willow, marjoram, and California poppy. These companions are useful for relaxing or getting to sleep if things get intense. They are not baneful and do not contain any narcotic properties. But that does not account for allergies, so please do your own research.

My favorite and most used combination for flying is two cocktails with only one ounce of alcohol per drink while smoking a combination of cannabis and mugwort. Then I lie down and enjoy.

History of Flying

In Rossell Robbins's *Encyclopedia of Witchcraft and Demonology*, flying is called *transvection*, which means the act of conveying or carrying over. In the encyclopedia's section under Ointments/Flying, Robbins discusses women in 1435 rubbing their bodies with an ointment. The encyclopedia states it was not until after this point in time that demonologists came to believe in witches physically flying.

The first known image of witches flying on broomsticks was later recorded in 1440. During this time, it was thought that witches flew to meet and make a compact with the devil. During the Inquisition in Southern France in the early 1500s, an inquisitor known as Avellaneda attended an inquisition meeting. In this meeting, the participants were trying to decide if witches physically flew. Six voted yes, three voted no, and two were undecided. This established a doubt about witches physically flying that has remained to this day.

In summary, you can now see how vast the beyond can be and how the various psychic skills are applied. The most important thing is to remain open, to not limit yourself to just what is known on Earth, but open yourself to the vast possibilities of the mind and beyond. Like my mom used to say, "All things are possible if you believe enough," so enjoy the journey.

Chapter 10
WHAT THEY DON'T TELL YOU

What I notice missing in most books on psychism is a conversation on how paradoxical psychism can be. Below are some of those paradoxes.

Once the door is open, it is open—which allows spontaneous events to occur. Equally, sometimes you can say no when you feel a psychic event is coming on and close the door. But this is not a 100 percent solution. Often the door you think you closed opens in your dreams later.

Typically, you are always right, until you are not—but then you find out later you were actually right.

People typically do not want someone to tell them the truth, even when they ask for it—nor do they typically listen to the truth when they hear it. Then they say, "Why didn't you tell me?" I used to call this the blessing and the curse of psychism and wondered, *Why have the skill then if this is true?* I have since discovered that when this occurs, the knowledge you have about what is to come is for you, so you can prepare for the fall out when things go wrong. It is a type of precognition as it were.

These paradoxes can make things difficult; however, there are several skills you can adapt to establish the boundaries between the real-world you, and your psychic self, to help ease the frustration.

PSYCHIC PARADOX SKILLS

The skills I speak of are compartmentalizing, detachment, dissociation, and self-compassion which is also called self-care.

In normal mental health models, these skills typically are used to help people recover from trauma. As a psychic I found it near impossible not to use these skills on a daily basis. They are part of our normal functions. So I decided I would embrace them as part of who I am and make them work for me as useful tools. I use them to reset my psyche and emotions after psychic events.

The skills discussed help psychics when they feel as though they have lived what they have experienced from a psychic event, which can leave the practitioner to deal with confusion and emotions that may not even be theirs. This creates dysphoria (confusion) and is why knowing your psychic self well, grounding, and self-care are vital after an event.

The human mind is an amazing thing. However, it does not know the difference between what you psychically see and experience and what your eyes see for real. You must be able to tell yourself which is which so the mind, emotions, and body can reset effectively. This takes compartmentalizing the information, detaching from the intensity, and then dissociating from the event. The process works in that order and helps the emotions brought on by a psychic event to be properly put in their place.

Living with psychism is much like living two lives and walking in two worlds. Usually, the recognition of the two-world thing, or that the stimuli do not belong to you, is all that is needed to reorient yourself. But if something is really intense, it takes a bit more work to put it in place.

If something has taken you by surprise or left you confused or blown away, stop whatever you are doing. Take time to pause and scan and figure out what you are feeling and why. If you are driving pull the car over until you have figured it out and regained yourself. This is the time for self-care. Nurture yourself.

While writing this book, I read through my journal. I came across the entry where my son died. As I read that entry, emotions welled up, which is to be expected. I had to pivot and remind myself now was not the time to revisit these emotions because I was working and had a goal in mind. After identifying the emotions, I compartmentalized them for later. I then detached from their intensity by using the stepping aside skill. Then I dissociated from the emotions by realizing they were not connected to the current moment. It helps knowing I can go back to them anytime I need to in a healthy manner.

Which is the second and most important part of this kind of work. For these skills to be healthy, you must go back later and address any leftover feelings. This takes discipline, effort, and much practice. Does it work every time? No; some things are so intense we are not given a choice but to deal with them right then. As with all the tools offered here, these are skills to use when we are able.

You do need to be watchful not to use them negatively. To use them in a negative manner would mean not going back and addressing your emotions later and just stuffing them.

The expert dreamer I often read about is Edgar Cayce, and he cautions not to get lost in the lure of the subconscious. I now caution you not to get lost in the lure of psychism. The following skills will assist in that too.

COMPARTMENTALIZING

In modern psychology, compartmentalizing is typically used to help people recover from trauma. However, for a psychic, it is a necessary tool sometimes used on a daily basis and it prevents us from burnout. We compartmentalize because our minds do not know the difference between psychic world experiences and the experiences you live daily unless you make sure it does. Compartmentalizing defines the difference and allows you to move past the psychic event and function daily in a normal manner.

How to Compartmentalize

To compartmentalize, you first must identify the item or subject you need to let go of. Here we are talking about psychic events like a precognitive vision that was disastrous and rocked you to the core while you were at work, things like that.

Then you need to figure out what feelings and emotions that are associated with that subject or item need to be let go of for now. For example, are you feeling breathless, sorrowful, overjoyed, blown away, devastated, or confused? These are the types of feelings that you need to let go of for now to function. Put them all in an inner visual box.

Next, you pick a time to go and unpack the box and keep that appointment. The box I put most of my stuff in is my journal. Later I will go back and read my journal and let myself feel, think about, and even discuss the event, process it more, and journal more about the processing.

Being aware that you just experienced something that was beyond your normal self helps the brain and emotions begin to reset to current reality. Which allows the brain to begin thinking rationally again. This shifts the brain from conceptual thinking back into linear thinking. Once the mind and emotions begin to relax the body will too.

If the event is intense, breathing and pivoting will bring you to a place where you can ground and center, compartmentalize, then move on with your day. Journaling is the best way I have found to fully compartmentalize an intense event. It is an act of putting it away firmly in a book to be dealt with later with detachment.

DETACHMENT

Detachment is a type of mental assertiveness that allows people to maintain their boundaries and psychic integrity when faced with emotional demands. Detachment is a decision to put away the item or subject until later and not think about it. Detachment in modern psychology means you have no emotional attachment to things or people. In psychism, you need to detach from the emotional impact of psychic events so that they do not overrun your normal functions. In this way, you can use detachment as a healthy tool and show yourself compassion.

Detachment allows you to look at your thoughts as an outsider and let them come and go. You do this without allowing yourself to feel too much about them, much like the observation skills learned in meditation. It is a choice to let it go for now without emotional reaction or involvement.

Detachment Practice

Think about an intense situation from your past and dredge up all the feelings of it. Now write the event down in your journal and include how you are currently feeling about it. Three days later go back to the journal and read the event and keep all feelings about the event closed off. Think only about what you may have learned from it or how it might help others.

Another way to practice detachment is to sit with someone who frustrates you. Sit face-to-face. Let them go first and allow them to say anything they wish to you. Your job is not to respond to any of it in any way. Then it is your turn to say what you wish to the other person. Their job is not to respond in any way. When you are done and alone, feel free to vent out loud to your pets or your pillow, then journal about it all. Leave all the feelings about it in your journal.

For those who have too much detachment and need to practice feeling more, use the wandering mind meditation and notice your feelings and let yourself feel them. Let yourself cry or be mad or happy—whatever comes—and journal about it. Set a timer for this work so you can get used to letting out feelings and then putting them back in the box when appropriate.

DISSOCIATION

Dissociation occurs when someone disconnects from some part of themselves or the environment. It can occur in several different ways, including disconnection from your own emotions, body sensations, memories, and senses. Dissociation can happen in mild forms even when there is no imminent danger or stress.

Think of a time you drove somewhere, arrived, and then could not remember the drive because your mind was wandering. Have you ever had an instance when you lost track of time because you were engrossed in a riveting television show? Those are forms of dissociation. Dissociation happens when you have disconnected from body sensations, like when you're on a tight deadline at work and you ignore being hungry or put off going to the bathroom.

Dissociation is something we all do, and it is a vital part of our ingrained survival system. It is a part of the system that helps us to cope with stressful situations that may otherwise feel overwhelming; it is built in but not pathological in nature. Dissociation in psychism allows us to put our events in the back of our memories where they will not interfere with normal thought processes. Later we can take things out of the box when appropriate.

Dissociation Practice

While experiencing something unpleasant, tell yourself, "This is not bothering me, I do not even notice," use the pause skill first, and *coach* yourself to not feel the feelings that would usually go with the experience and breathe. Tell yourself that pushing this aside is just temporary. The stepping aside skill is important to this work.

SELF-COMPASSION/SELF-CARE

The typical definition of compassion is showing or having care and concern for others. In psychism, the compassion we show is for ourselves. It involves being gentle with yourselves and using self-care emotionally, physically, and psychically. Self-nurturing is the best thing you can do for yourself.

Many individuals find it difficult to give to themselves or take time for themselves, I am no different. We are socially conditioned to take care of everything else first. Compassion for ourselves is taking that five or ten minutes we need to do creative pursuits we enjoy and putting off our other duties for a short time. Self-compassion is taking time to live, love, and laugh, and keep healthy boundaries. These things need to be just as, if not more, important to us than our obligations and comittments.

Not using compartmentalizing, detachment, dissociation, and self-compassion can lead to mental harm, leaving you feeling drained, exhausted, traumatized, or even depressed. However, we must use these sparingly and not overindulge ourselves. Using them too often can result in not living our lives to the fullest.

For psychics, the more involved with this world we are, the less we hear, feel, or see the psychic world. This is why striking a balance between self-knowledge and self-care needs to become a way of living.

SPONTANEOUS EVENTS

Spirits come to those who are open to hearing them whether you realize you are open or not. It does not matter if you are busy, or if you realize you are open at the time. This too is a paradox of psychism.

Many writers speak about grounding and shielding before conducting any psychic work and having control. However, psychic events do not only happen with intent and in controlled environments. Spontaneous events happen all the time with no grounding or shielding. Shielding and grounding keep you and your space protected when you can do it, but it cannot stop a spontaneous event from happening, nor can it keep the psychic experience a nice, happy experience. This is because psychism only works when you are completely open to receiving stimuli.

Effective shielding and control during a spontaneous event come psychically in the moment of need as things occur, from inside your mind. The best protection a psychic has with spontaneous events is knowing their psychic self and mundane self extremely well. You must be very skilled in bringing up a psychic shield in your mind with just a thought.

Psychic shields can be an actual shield, a powerful emanation of energy directed with your hand or an object you hold, the thought of "I reject or repel this, go away," or even a command voice of *stop* or *no* or a mirror you mentally flash up.

These inner psychic skills come from a practice in trance work and learning to control your dreams. If you can control your dreams and protect yourself there, you have the skill to bring up a psychic shield when needed during a spontaneous event.

The psychics who deal with spontaneous events the most are those who feel they were born with psychic skills and never had to practice to achieve these skills.

I have often had psychic information come in the middle of a sentence while talking to someone. Usually, it makes me look up or turn my head and listen a moment, which is my tell, I suppose. Sometimes I try to listen to both things at once, and sometimes that works. But typically, the psychic information is stronger, and I stop hearing the person I am with. Then I must turn to them and say, "I am sorry, what was that?" It may look odd to a person not familiar with psychism. Sometimes, even if they are familiar with psychism, they get annoyed because I am not paying attention. So I make what amends I can, given the situation. This is how I deal with spontaneous events in public. Most people think I am just distracted or scatter-brained, and that is okay. It is part of living two lives at once.

Then there is dealing with the two sides of accuracy in a social context because sometimes you are right and sometimes you are not. This is difficult for everyone on both sides of this issue. Sometimes you get scoffed at and sometimes you blow people's minds or even scare them with your skill. This can leave you and others feeling awkward and unsure of you and your skills.

I used to fuss a lot about how inconsistent my skills were. Now I am glad they ebb and flow and I think of them as giving me a break. I do not think the human mind can stand having its full psychic skills on all the time. I have met a few people who have that problem, and I usually recommend medication to quiet these folks temporarily. Another issue for psychics is that we are both vessels and human, and we need to remember to take care of our human self.

Spontaneous events while driving, however, are a whole other deal. Most are mild and result in me looking like I am talking to myself. A few have made me pull over, or lose time, or forget how I got where I am going. All of this can lead to making excuses, and hiding ourselves and our needs in front of others, especially if we are late or in the middle of something.

The skills in this chapter help us deal with spontaneous events, not only as a way of coping with what we experience but for daily function as we deal with living with the two worlds we experience when we cross the hedge, cross the veil, do trance work, practice Magic, and deal with our social circles.

Another paradox that many psychics struggle with is that the more involved you are with the world, the more your psychic skills decline or take a back seat. Yet it is this world that requires our skills. I find that the busier I am with work or other obligations, the more my skills ebb or get cloudy. It is for this reason that I and many psychics lead an alternative lifestyle in order to maintain a functional mental-emotional balance to keep their skills active while keeping themselves productive in society. Through self-exploration, journaling, and self-understanding, this book will help you find what works best for you, and your experiences and struggles. As you do the work and have experiences, it is helpful to remember that there is always more that is hidden and waiting to be discovered.

Chapter 11
THE HIDDEN PSYCHIC

I discovered the hidden psychic phenomenon when I was working as a Dual Diagnosis counselor, which is a counselor of people who have both mental health issues and an addiction.

During my fifteen years of working with the people on the streets, in the detox, methadone clinics, and among those of the Native Nations, I began to see a pattern and started to keep records of my findings. It proved that 40 percent of the clientele that I saw in my time actually had spiritual, religious, or psychic issues, not mental health issues, and they were self-medicating to manage.

THE HIDDEN PSYCHIC

There are many people who have had spontaneous events who do not even know they are psychics. These folks are typically led to believe, or may fear, they have mental health issues. Approximately 40 percent of my clients had experienced spontaneous events since they could remember without knowing what those events were. Which means they were likely born a psychic, a witch, a profit, a seer, a messenger, or a magical practitioner of some kind and had no idea; they just felt lost, confused, and ungrounded. Many just felt wrong, broken, or out of control.

THE MARGINALIZED

Once I created a relationship of trust and safety, I was able to gently introduce the concepts of psychism when I felt it applied to the situation. I always started with intuition because that is the most socially acceptable term for anything psychic. Approaching psychism with more acceptable terms allowed folks to feel comfortable and expressive with their issues. My clinical work became the creating and testing ground for many of the exercises in this book. It is what motivated me to leave the clinic and its restrictions and become a spiritual teacher and guide. I knew I could reach more people on the street level. I spent time listening to the people I encountered and found they had many feelings or beliefs in common.

The most prominent feelings and beliefs that were expressed in my work are listed here:

"You feel and know things others do not but you are afraid to speak up." This means that there is a part of them they keep hidden and they go through life feeling like they cannot really be or express their true selves. They live in fear of honest expression.

"You feel everything from everywhere and cannot sort it out, and I know I am not autistic so I must be crazy and need to be drugged, right?"

"Knowing early you do not belong or fit in."

"Always having to hide or hold back a part of yourself. Not ever having anyone you trust to talk to."

"Fear of being locked up if you did speak up."

"Having one side of the family be encouraging and the other awful and demeaning."

"Being a social outcast."

"Self-medicating or hanging with the wrong crowd just to feel like you belong somewhere."

"I am afraid they will lock me up if I ever tell someone about the voices." The voices referred to here are the voices when spirits and deities speak to us in pathworking, visions, dreams, or trance.

"At a young age I realized I was hypersensitive to my surroundings."

I bet many can relate to some of these feelings and beliefs. I sure did as I grew up. For those who do not identify or understand what these feelings are like, imagine waking up as a six year old, naked in front of your first-grade class. You are scared, vulnerable, and confused, and you definitely know you do not belong. Sounds terrifying, right? That is how many psychics feel most of their lives, especially if they have no clue they are psychic. The feelings and beliefs they have in common are how many identify with their hypersensitivity to their surroundings.

THE PSYCHIC AMPLIFIER EFFECT

Because psychics are hypersensitive to their surroundings, they know when another psychic is in proximity. I call it the *amplifier effect* and it is an interesting phenomenon. They may not know specifically, but they can feel "something" that puts them on high alert.

The amplifier effect is where we can see the real law of attraction play out before our very eyes as we watch the actions of the psychic. Below is the science behind it, using the example of the law of attraction from chapter 3.

When two psychics are close to each other, their field of thoughts and energy atoms become excited. They are stimulated by another field that is similar to theirs. It's the feeling we get when we think we have found our soul mate or feel we are kindred to someone we just met. However, for a psychic, as the friendship progresses, the atom fields continue to get stimulated and amplify the psychic field around the two psychics, and the two surround fields join. When they do, they become a stronger psychic energy, and typically maintain a psychic link no matter how far in distance they get from each other.

This typically amplifies the psychic abilities through the now shared field. This can happen with most anyone as long as the vibrations each is emitting are similar.

I see this effect play out with my husband and me. His empath skills are stronger than mine. However, as we live together, occasionally it is difficult for us to know whose emotion or thought originated with whom. We will both feel it originated within us. My son and I made a game of it called "Whose thought is it anyway?"

The amplification effect has even occurred with my roommate and other good friends who are psychic. This occurs because once the atom surround fields connect, they become familiar and are happy to interact with each other over and over, like brain synapses seeking out the pleasure centers. This is the law of attraction in its purest form. Many feel it is something they cannot help. Well, yes and no. Like emotions, we still will have the emotion, but we can choose how to react, and to connect or not. If the psychic applies awareness to the pull or flash of the connection as it is occurring, then the five faculties of the mind can be applied and allow the psychic to choose how to respond and get a better grip on their senses.

THE EMOTIONAL CONNECTION

Another hidden factor to psychism is the emotional connection. We have seen how an emotional connection can cause people to exhibit extraordinary feats of strength. We see hints of this in the psychic world but only through movies such as *Firestarter*, *Poltergeist*, and *X-Men*. What they show in those films is only one aspect of the emotional connection and they are correct in that moments of duress or anger can drastically increase a psychic ability, but not to the level in the films.

I have experienced emotional anger or duress and used a command voice in the real world and in the beyond. The command of *stop* coupled with an intense emotional psychic desire and vision is enough to stop most anyone. Couple an intense command such as *Stop*, *I wouldn't*, or *Don't* with the "Mom" look and a hand movement and it is usually enough to freeze most people or animals in their tracks. Using it in dreams and on the astral only intensifies its effectiveness.

This emotional connection is the reason many of the myths of psychism are created. Psychics are told they have to be in control, that it is dangerous not to be in control, or to only do psychism in a controlled setting with training. Those of us who experience spontaneous events know how impossible it is to meet those restrictions all the time, and those restrictions only serve to marginize us further.

Emotional psychism used under duress or fear resonates in the high frequencies of vibration and energy. When you analyze such an event, you will realize the energy and vibration was so strong it was felt in your body and traveled through the body of the receiver. This odd vibrational sensation moving through them is what stops most people. They pause, unsure about what they just felt. In addition, their mind cannot process it fast enough because it is so unfamiliar. So they stop and think, What was that? Without even knowing that is what they were thinking. They only know they suddenly feel perplexed for a moment.

It is precisely because there is an emotional connection coming and going that psychism works. The other emotional connection is the one between those closest to you. This connection develops over time and resonates on a lower and deeper set of frequencies that can be felt. These frequencies are comfortable to the body and mind. They feel like they are supposed to be there and when they are disrupted the psychic notices. I call it my radar. It too can be felt in the body by the sender and the receiver, sometimes at a great distance and through dreams. These connections are what make psychic sex possible between very connected people or can be drawn on for magical support or emotional strength during a trance or dream. This kind of connection gets activated just by thinking of the person or when they think of you, you can feel it. This type of emotional connection is responsible for events like "I was just thinking of you!" or knowing when someone is sick or troubled.

There is so much in psychism that is variable and undefinable, or simply unique to the individual or circumstance that it is impossible to cover it all. The best way to discover and define your own skill is to make a lifetime study of it. This is done by recording every event you can, journaling, studying your notes, and researching.

This all brings us to the last paradox of psychism and the reason for this book.

There are so many psychics who are marginalized, feel they cannot speak up, or feel they are alone and no one understands. Yet, there exists a wide world of public psychics who have been practicing for a long time. Just look up "psychic institutes" and you will see you are not alone.

We are many and we are waiting for you.

BIBLIOGRAPHY

Andrews, Ted. *How to Do Psychic Readings Through Touch.* Woodbury, MN: Llewellyn Worldwide, 2005.

Blair, Lawrence. *Rhythms of Vision: The Changing Patterns of Belief.* New York: Warner Books, 1997.

Bletzer, June G. *The Donning International Encyclopedic Psychic Dictionary.* West Chester, PA: Schiffer Publishing, 1986.

Bonewits, Phaedra, and Isaac Bonewits. *Real Energy: Systems, Spirits, and Substances to Heal, Change, and Grow.* Franklin Lakes, NJ: The Career Press, 2007.

Boswell, Harriet A. *Master Guide to Psychism.* West Nyack, NY: Parker Publishing, 1969.

Bradley, Marion Zimmer. *The Mists of Avalon.* New York: Ballantine Publishing, 1982.

Cayce, Edgar. *The Power of Your Mind.* Virginia Beach, VA: A.R.E. Press, 2010.

———. *The Psychic Sense.* Virginia Beach, VA: A.R.E. Press, 2006.

Freud, Sigmund. *On Dreams.* Introduction by Leslie Mackenzie. Translated by M. D. Eder. Overland Park, KS: Digi-reads Publishing, 2019.

Frost, Gavin, and Yvonne Frost. *Astral Travel: Your Guide to the Secrets of Out-Of-The-Body Experiences.* Great Britain: Granada Publishing, 1982.

———. *The Magic Power of Witchcraft.* West Nyack, NY: Parker Publishing Company, 1977.

———. *Meta-Psychometry: Key to Power and Abundance.* West Nyack, NY: Parker Publishing Company, 1978.

Gandhi, Mahatma. *The Story of My Experiments with the Truth: Mahatma Gandhi's Unabridged Autobiography.* Edited by Advano Lucchese. Valley Cottage, NY: Discovery Publisher, 2018.

Gurney, Edmund. *Phantasms of the Living.* London: Forgotten Books, 2015.

Haining, Peter. *The Anatomy of Witchcraft.* New York: Taplinger Publishing, 1972.

Hall, Jamie A. *Jungian Dream Interpretation: A Study in Jung.* Toronto: Inner City Books, 1983.

Hobson, Allan J. *Dreaming as Delirium: How the Brain Goes Out.* Boston: Little Brown, 1994.

Jung, Carl G. *Synchronicity: An Acasual Connecting Principle,* volume 8, *Collected Works of C. G. Jung.* Translation by R. F. C. Hull. Princeton, NJ: Princeton University Press, 2010

Leek, Sybil. *The Sybil Leek Book of Fortune Telling.* Toronto: Macmillan Company, 1969.

———. *Telepathy.* New York: Macmillan Company, 1971.

Lethbridge, T. C. *ESP Beyond Time and Distance.* London: Sidgwick & Jackson, 1974.

MacQuarrie, Charles W. *The Biography of the Irish God of the Sea: From the Voyage of Bran the Waves of Manannan.* Lewiston, NY: Edwin Millen Press, 2004.

Monroe, Robert A. *Journeys Out of the Body.* New York: Doubleday, 1971.

———. *The Ultimate Journey.* New York: Doubleday, 1994.

Murphy, Joseph. *The Power of Your Subconscious Mind*. Englewood Cliffs, NJ: Prentice Hall, 1974.

Orloff, Judith. *Second Sight*. New York: Warner Books, 1996.

Peach, Edward. *The Art and Practice of Clairvoyance*. New York: Samuel Weiser, 1975.

Peirce, Penny. *The Intuitive Way*. New York: MJF Books, 1997.

Pinch, Geraldine. *Egyptian Mythology: A Guide to the Gods, Goddesses, and Traditions of Ancient Egypt*. New York: Oxford Press, 2004.

Pollack, Jack Harrison. *Croiset: The Clairvoyant*. New York: Bantam Books, 1965.

Rasbold, Katrina. *Crossroads and Conjure*. Woodbury, MN: Llewellyn Publications, 2009.

Ridgeway, Anrei. *Psychic Living: Tap into Your Psychic Potential*. Barnes and Noble Press, 2000.

Robbins, Rossell Hope. *The Encyclopedia of Witchcraft and Demonology*. New York: Crown Publishers, 1959.

Scott, Michael. *Delphi: A History of the Center of the Ancient World*. Princeton, NJ: Princeton University Press, 2016.

Sechrist, Elsie. *Dreams: Your Magic Mirror*. New York: Cowles Education Corporation, 1968.

Tolle, Eckhart. *A New Earth: Awakening to Your Life's Purpose*. New York: Penguin Group, 2006.

———. *The Power of Now: A Guide to Spiritual Enlightenment*. Novato, CA: New World Library, 2004.

Ullman, Montague, and Stanley Krippner. *Dream Telepathy*. New York: Macmillan, 1973.

Weschcke, Carl Llewellyn, and Joe H. Slate. *Clairvoyance for Psychic Empowerment: The Art & Science of "Clear Seeing" Past the*

Illusions of Space & Time & Self Deception. Woodbury, MN: Llewellyn Publications, 2013.

Zell-Ravenheart, Oberon. *Grimoire for the Apprentice Wizard*. Franklin Lakes, NJ: Career Press, 2004.

Zolar. *The Encyclopedia of Ancient and Forbidden Knowledge*. Los Angeles: Nash Publishing, 1970.

INDEX

TO WRITE TO THE AUTHOR

If you wish to contact the author or would like more information about this book, please write to the author in care of Llewellyn Worldwide Ltd. and we will forward your request. Both the author and publisher appreciate hearing from you and learning of your enjoyment of this book and how it has helped you. Llewellyn Worldwide Ltd. cannot guarantee that every letter written to the author can be answered, but all will be forwarded. Please write to:

Cat Gina Cole
℅ Llewellyn Worldwide
2143 Wooddale Drive
Woodbury, MN 55125-2989

Please enclose a self-addressed stamped envelope for reply, or $1.00 to cover costs. If outside the U.S.A., enclose an international postal reply coupon.

Many of Llewellyn's authors have websites with additional information and resources. For more information, please visit our website at http://www.llewellyn.com.

NOTES

NOTES

NOTES

NOTES